Playing the Field

Algonquin Books of Chapel Hill   1987

Jim Kaplan

Playing the Field

with an introduction by Dick Howser

published by
Algonquin Books of Chapel Hill
Post Office Box 2225
Chapel Hill, North Carolina 27515–2225

in association with
Taylor Publishing Company
1550 West Mockingbird Lane
Dallas, Texas 75235

Portions of this book appeared in *Sports Illustrated*, *Sport*, and *The National Pastime*.

Excerpts from *Portnoy's Complaint* by Philip Roth in Chapter 12 reprinted by permission of Random House, Inc., copyright © 1967 by Philip Roth.

We are indebted to the following organizations and persons for the photographs appearing in this book, which are used with their permission: Pat Kelly, National Baseball Library, Cooperstown, New York; Matthew L. Kaplan, New York, N.Y.; California Angels; Pittsburgh Pirates; San Diego Padres; Philadelphia Phillies; New York Yankees; Baltimore Orioles; Oakland Athletics; Boston Red Sox; Atlanta Braves; San Francisco Giants; Detroit Tigers; and UPI/Bettmann Archives.

LIBRARY OF CONGRESS CATALOGING-IN-PUBLICATION DATA
Kaplan, Jim.
  Playing the field.
  1. Baseball—United States. 2. Baseball players—United
States—Interviews. I. Title.
GV863.A1K36   1987   796.357'0973   86-28696
ISBN 0-912697-36-9

To my sons, Benjamin and Matthew

Contents

List of Illustrations

Introduction: The Necessity of Defense

by Dick Howser

There has never been a good baseball team that was not strong defensively. You used to be able to afford below-average left-fielders and rightfielders, but now you need good range at those positions because on artificial turf everyone's running. I look for good range and a quick, accurate release more than I look for a strong arm. There are a lot of ways to compensate for a below-average arm, but not for a lack of speed. If you don't go get the ball, the opponents will run you out of the ballpark. Since the runners are so fast, it's also more important than ever to know how to position your fielders and pitch to the hitters.

In 1985 we had to be especially strong in the field because we didn't score a lot of runs. If you don't score much, you can't afford to allow many runs. People say the up-the-middle positions are most important, and I believe it. The Royals have been contenders for the past decade or so in part because they've been strong at catcher, short, second, and center. All the great Yankee and Oriole teams were like that. The catcher can maneuver people, infielders move around the shortstop and second baseman, and the outfielders work around the center-fielder. Just look at the guys we had in those positions when we won the Series. Our centerfielder, Willie Wilson, got as good a jump on fly balls as anyone—I still can't believe a ball he ran down off Ozzie Smith. Our catcher, Jim Sundberg, handled pitchers well and used his terrific arm. Frank White fielded perfectly. They talked about Buddy Biancalana's batting and on-base percentage. Well, don't forget his play at short. Over two seven-game series, he outplayed Tony Fernandez of the Blue Jays and Ozzie Smith of the Cardinals, two of the best in the business.

Every day in spring training we work on defensive fundamentals. Most of our guys are experienced, but we go over fundamentals as a reminder. Take the relays. We practice them on balls hit down the right-field line, over the rightfielder's head, to right-center, over the centerfielder's head. We practice them with nobody on base, a runner on first, runners on first and second. We use what we call a double cutoff, with both the shortstop and second baseman running into the outfield and one backing up the other. A good relay system helps prevent opponents from taking the extra bases that decide games.

We'll also practice defensing the plays that teams use with men on first and third: the double steal, delayed steal, forced balk. What people don't understand about the double steal is that we're not as concerned about getting the guy at second as we are preventing the guy at third from scoring. If the man on first steals second, first is open and we can pitch around the batter or walk the guy to set up a force. So when the man on first runs, we have several variations: throw through to a fielder at second who comes up throwing to third, throw to the middle infielder cutting behind the pitcher's mound, throw to third for a pickoff. We also have to worry about what to do if the runner stops between first and second. We're constantly practicing rundowns. If we're not doing them right, we might practice them on an off-day during the season.

We spend as much fielding practice with our pitchers as our everyday players. In addition to that familiar 3-1 play where the pitcher covers first on grounders, we practice holding runners, pitching out, working pickoffs. The pitcher has to learn to throw to first a lot and vary his timing to keep the runner off-stride. The throw to second is strictly a timing play between the pitcher and fielder—that's why you go over it again and again and again. It's important for pitchers to hold runners and field their position—the little things. They didn't have many runners in school and the minors. Even Dwight Gooden was below average at holding runners when he made the majors.

It's not always a big hit that wins a game, but it's often a defensive play. And it's not so much having good defensive players as guys who are in proper position. Before every series I go over hitters with the catcher, and one of our coaches, Billy Gardner, talks with the shortstop, second baseman, and centerfielder. During the game Billy is in charge of moving these players around. The players always move together. If, say, the center-fielder moves to left-center, the leftfielder moves toward the line and the rightfielder to right-center. If the shortstop moves in the hole, the second baseman moves closer to the bag.

I've got hitting charts on opponents that go back to 1980. What's on them? The ballpark, its dimensions, what pitch was hit, where it was in the strike zone, the count, whether it was a ground ball, a routine fly, a hard-hit fly. Say a righthanded hit-ter hits a ball to right-center. Was it a breaking ball away, a fast-ball on his hands, a pitch up or down in the strike zone; did he hit a looper into right field or hit it with authority? Maybe he hit a mistake pitch; in that case, we won't have to adjust the next time. If he keeps pounding the ball out there, he's a right-center hitter. Before he learned how to pull, we gave Kirby Puckett, the Twins' righthanded hitting centerfielder, the left field line and had our shortstop almost behind second. Our charts showed that he hit to the right side and up the middle. Now that he swings differently, we need new charts. I like ex-tensive charts. Once a guy has batted 40 or 50 times against us, we have something to work with. Another thing about charts: they're a check on your memory. Here's what I mean. Every fielder remembers the hits that beat him. "Last time through, this guy beat me on a hit up the middle," a shortstop will say, arguing in favor of moving to his left when the hitter comes up. But the charts will show that most of the time the guy pulls the ball. Percentages don't lie, and we play them. If a new guy comes into the league and there's no book on him, I'll talk to other managers or minor league managers who have worked against him.

We have a computer service that gives us what a guy's hitting against various pitchers, how he's doing in day games and night games and in various ballparks—that kind of thing. But a computer can't replace what you see for yourself. If George Brett is hot, a printout of past performances won't help much. You have to have a feeling whether a player's hot or cold, or if he has a fast bat or a slow bat. Computers also don't give you the most current information: whether a pitcher is going well or has a blister on his finger or is sick. If Dan Quisenberry is pitching for us, I usually have a feeling where the batter is going to hit the ball that a computer can't give me. Dan's not going to pitch to their power, and the batter is probably going

Paul Blair's great catch of George Scott's drive in 1974.
Baltimore Orioles

to hit the ball on the ground. All we can hope is that we're play-ing the guy right, and he hits it to us. Baseball is not a com-puter game.

I'm constantly on the phone with our advance scout, Al Diez, who is watching most of the teams we'll play in the next series. He calls me from hotel rooms and airports. I ask him questions like, "How are Dwight Evans and Rich Gedman swinging the bat? Has a guy got a bad thumb so he can't turn on the ball?" Al will tell me, "They've got this new young outfielder who probably just plays against lefthanders. They'll pinch-hit with him late in the game. He'll steal second but not third. They won't hit-and-run with this pinch hitter, but they may with this other." That's the kind of information I need. I'll ask him, "Al, what's Jack Morris's out pitch? Is he throwing the forkball as much as he used to? What will Walt Terrell throw you with two strikes and two outs and a lefthanded hitter versus a right-handed hitter?"

You want to know which clubs work first-and-third situa-tions, so you can pitch out to them. You want to know which

Dick Howser. *Kansas City Royals*

ones squeeze a lot, so you can pitch out or throw them high, inside pitches that are tough to bunt. Maybe I learn a guy isn't pulling as much as he did. We have to play him straight-up. Is a guy off the bench a first-ball hitter? Is he up there trying to take a walk? Some come up there swinging, others want to measure a fastball. If we arrive in Boston Sunday night, the reports from that day's game are waiting for me. Again, that's the kind of thing computers can't give you.

We don't give our guys playbooks to study over the winter because I think it's important for them to get away from the game. They learn or review what they need to in spring training. We try to do everything the same way all through our farm system. That's why we bring the minor leaguers to Fort Myers for the first 10 days of spring training. Before every practice I sit down with the coaches and tell them how I want to practice fundamentals that day. I want them especially to do things the way we do at Double-A Memphis and Triple-A Omaha—the higher classifications.

Basketball coaches talk about how players move without the

ball. We're the same way in baseball. I saw one play by another team in spring training that turned my stomach. There was a man on second and a base hit to center field. The centerfielder came up throwing home. Fair enough. Only the first baseman was not where he was supposed to be: at the pitcher's mound to make the cutoff. The throw was a little up the third-base line, and the cutoff man, who was still on his way to the mound from first, didn't reach it. As a result, the run scored and the batter reached second. No error, just a dumb play. A team like the Orioles, on the other hand, will have their cutoff men lined up exactly between the outfielder and the plate. That's one reason why statistics don't tell you everything you need to know about defense. You have to be there watching the little things.

I haven't sat down and thought about an all-time all-star team, but I can tell you about some players who got my attention over an extended period. The best third basemen I ever saw were Clete Boyer and Brooks Robinson. The best shortstop was Luis Aparicio; they called him "the bandit" because he stole so many hits. I probably idolized him more than anyone else because he was my size and played my position. He made every kind of play. The one he handled best was a topped ball over the mound with a guy on first. He'd field it and flip back to second for the force. At second base there have been a lot of good ones, like Bobby Richardson and Bill Mazeroski, but Frank White may be as good as anyone. Del Crandall and Mike Hegan were fine first basemen, and I'm told Mike's father Jim was as great a catcher. The Yankees always had good catchers: Yogi Berra, Elston Howard, Ralph Houk, and Charlie Silvera, to name some of them in my time. Paul Blair was as good as anyone I've seen in center because he played so shallow. He had the courage and instinct to play that way, and he saved a lot of bloopers. I don't think I ever saw a ball that went over his head and stayed in the ballpark, except maybe a line drive off the fence. Al Kaline in right was maybe the best I ever saw at throwing out a runner going from first to third on a base hit. He came after the ball like a shortstop.

It's interesting: Carl Yastrzemski and Blair were also signed as shortstops. Now that I think of it, some of the best preparation for outfield might be playing infield. You're never too old to learn something new about fielding.

Preface

It is a moment frozen in time and space. The year: 1968. The place: a Minneapolis softball diamond. The position: center field.

The ball shoots off the bat, streaks past the infield, and takes off into the air like a comet. "Joltin' Joe," I whisper, turning on my heels. "The Gray Eagle. Say, hey." With my back to home plate, I race to the point where I know the ball will land; Joe DiMaggio, Tris Speaker, and Willie Mays would have done no less. I turn at the last instant, extend a gloved hand, and—thwapp!—make the catch of my life. It's the last out of the inning, and as I jog back to the bench, both teams are on their feet applauding. I smile broadly. I'm actually having a modestly good time.

My happiest moments in baseball were always in the field. I remember those practices in the seventh grade. I was a catcher, and I loved wearing all that heavy equipment, sweating heavily for the first time, getting dirty—really dirty. I never did learn to catch the ball when the batter swung and missed. By contrast right field, where I played in the games, was a wonderful place to daydream. The other positions would prove to be every bit as unique and interesting. You have your memories, I have mine. Second base was where Jonathan Lebedoff and Phil Gainsley, two putative friends whom I'd introduced to the Chilmark, Massachusetts, softball game, had the temerity to rob me of base hits. Third was where I wowed 'em at the *Sports Illustrated* outing. Left was where I fell asleep and misplayed Nat Bowditch's easy liner; no practical navigator, I dropped it for a clear E7. First was where I turned Norman Maida's screeching rope into a one-man double play. Short could only have been manned by little Bumpy Wyzanski. Above all, positions are personalities.

All my life I've loved the geometry of the nine positions and their interrelatedness in a scorebook.[1] My favorites were always glovemen: New York Governor Mario Cuomo (a better centerfielder than hitter in the Pirate farm system), Ozzie Smith, Bill Mazeroski. For some reason, I like Italian-surnamed third basemen: Frank Malzone, Sal Bando, Ron Santo, Doug DeCinces. And I have special fondness for players like Greg Pryor and Bob Bailor whose fielding helped keep them in the majors.

I was a natural sucker for fielding by process of elimination: I couldn't throw strikes or hit the ball very far over the infield. What I've discovered in researching this book, however, is that people far more proficient at pitching and hitting feel exactly the same way as I do about defense. One of my friends, Jim Reynolds, was a Belmont Hill School pitcher good enough to be recruited by several colleges. "What I really enjoyed," he says, "was playing third base when I wasn't pitching. I loved to field those quick hoppers and just stand there. The batter probably thought he had it made. Then I'd hitch, cock, and throw the bum out." Another buddy, Nicky Dawidoff, was a hitting star at old Hopkins Grammar School in New Haven. What Nicky really enjoyed, though, was playing shortstop. "It's so fluid, so much constant movement. You always get to show your range. And I love that throw from the hole, where you can release the ball, really air it out."

The truth is, almost everyone enjoys playing the field. Nevertheless, when I looked into a book on the subject, I found that virtually no authors had explored the subject except to write instructionals. My task seemed simple enough: write about the best fielders, rate the positions, describe the best plays in the biggest games. I quickly became diverted. The best players, I learned soon enough, do not always coincide with the most interesting ones. Although there's considerable overlap on the following pages, be forewarned: this book contains an all-interesting team, not necessarily an all-all-star team.

How does one even begin to rate the positions? I mean, is catcher or shortstop the toughest? I decided that shortstop was the hardest "fielding" position (i.e., a shortstop has more difficult plays on batted balls than anyone else), catcher the toughest "defensive" position (the scope of his duties and difficulties

---

1. If you're keeping score, pitcher is represented by 1, catcher 2, first base 3, second base 4, third base 5, shortstop 6, left field 7, center field 8, and right field 9.

is unmatched). I further concluded that the second baseman has a greater variety of challenges than shortstop, that third basemen probably make more game-saving stops than anyone, that first base is the most underrated position on the field, and that everyone, including the centerfielder himself, says that the position where I became a softball immortal isn't as tough as commonly thought. So the list would look something like this:

1. Catcher and shortstop (tie). How's that for a copout?

3. Second base. Hey, *you* try making the pivot.

4. Third base. An awful lot of games turn on those drives down the left-field line.

5. First base! A lot of games turn on those scoops too.

6. Center field. Historically overrated, but still the toughest position in the outfield.

7. Right field. Only the lower number of chances make right easier than center. Right is also the position I found most fascinating. It's my personal favorite—for reasons other than daydreaming.

8. Left field. Now and always, primarily a hitter's position.

9. Pitcher.

But isn't the pitcher in a sense the most important defensive player—the one who initiates all play, limits or expands the work duty of his brethren? I decided that rating the positions was of small consequence. Describing them in detail would be more interesting.

It was easy to find the best plays in Series games and pennant races. Visiting the Hall of Fame, I found another world of equally meritorious but less celebrated plays in little-noted games. The Hall's estimable publicist, Bill Guilfoile, had put out the word to Famer and fan alike: send me your poor, your tired, your huddled fielding plays yearning to breathe the fresh air of celebrity. I began poring over his list of 150-odd submissions. "You are the first journalist ever to look through this file," Guilfoile told me. I was thrilled. Even as Alex Haley's ancestors had spoken to him from the water in *Roots*, I felt myself summoned by generations of fielding gems.

None of which compares to my moment in center.

Jim Kaplan

Acknowledgments

I have many people to thank. John Thorn, the coauthor (with Pete Palmer) of *The Hidden Game of Baseball*, supplied most of my historical information, scrutinized the manuscript, and answered my constant calls without the least exasperation. Ira Berkow, Steve Wulf, Audrey McGinn, Brooks Robards, and my mother, Felicia Lamport Kaplan, had helpful suggestions about form and content. Publicist Bill Guilfoile, librarian Tom Heitz, and photo collection manager Pat Kelly were invaluable when I visited the Hall of Fame. Lloyd Johnson, the executive director of the Society for American Baseball Research (SABR), sent me research material. Jack Etkin, Warner Fuselle, David Fisher, Henry Hecht, Paul Ladewski, Adam Mansbach, and Allan Zullo supplied useful quotes and anecdotes. Nicky Dawidoff, Jim Reynolds, and David Sparrow checked the manuscript and expunged inaccuracies and rhetorical leaps stretched to the point of hamstring pulls. And lastly, some old (and young) reliables: my son Matthew, who suggested the book and took many photographs for it; Ted Stephney, who processed Matthew's pictures; my other son Benjamin, who never once complained when I kept heading for the ballpark instead of the beach in spring training; Robert Creamer, who alerted me to the blessed existence of Algonquin Books of Chapel Hill; my agent, Dominick Abel, and my redoubtable publisher, Louis D. Rubin, Jr. If I've forgotten any other worthies, I owe you a ballpark hot dog.

Playing the Field

1

In Defense of Defense

On April 28, 1978, a 23-year-old San Diego Padres shortstop named Ozzie Smith came of age. The Braves' Jeff Burroughs hit a hard grounder up the middle, and Smith broke hard to his left and dived. While he was airborne and horizontal, the ball kicked to his right, leaving him in the apparently hopeless position of a man jumping into an unfilled swimming pool. No matter. Smith reached back and barehanded the ball, bounced off the ground like a gymnast off a trampoline, and threw out the runner. The sequence was flash-danced across the country on the weekly TV highlight film, and America was introduced to the greatest fielder in the game today.

Baseball was invented as a fielding game. The defense was given the ball, the purpose was to put it in play, and the most cherished skill was fielding ability. Today fans like to see the ball hit out of the park; Alexander Cartwright, who established the original 1845 rules, wanted it to be kept in. Indeed, he ordered balls clearing the field fair or foul to be considered foul! "The best player in a nine is he who makes the most good plays in a match," wrote Henry Chadwick, the game's first great thinker. There were innumerable opportunities for fielding gems. Balls and strikes weren't called until the 1860s, pitchers weren't allowed to throw with a bent wrist until 1872, the overhand delivery wasn't legalized until 1884, and hitters could call for high or low pitches until 1887. Unfortunately, fielders rarely distinguished themselves. They wore no gloves and had so much trouble catching the ball that they were given outs on one-bounce flies until 1864. (A notable exception was an outfielder named John Chapman, who was called "death to flying things" for his ability to make one-handed and over-the-shoulder catches.)

Alas, even as conditions improved for the fielders, hitting and pitching took over the game. From the late 1850s until the early 1860s Jim Creighton, a pitcher for the Brooklyn Excelsiors, threw with speed and spin and an imperceptible wrist flip that created the illusion of a rising fastball; he was virtually unhittable. In later years the hitters rebounded: when the pitcher was moved from 45 to 50 feet from home in 1881, when four strikes were allowed in 1887, and especially when the pitcher was moved farther back in 1893 and permanently located at 60 feet, six inches from the plate. That season the National League batting average shot up from .245 to .280.

The fielder? Hand-sized gloves were first used in 1875, but there followed sporadic attempts to abolish or limit the damn things because they made fielding too easy! It wasn't until the 1890s that gloves were large enough to catch balls as well as protect hands from injuries. Fielding skill was still prized until the 1920s, when Babe Ruth and the lively ball forever shifted attention to the hitter-pitcher duel. Fielding never caught up. It was so taken for granted that until 1954 players left their priceless gloves on the outfield grass when they were hitting. The only major award given fielders—the Gold Glove—wasn't issued until 1957. Today sluggers and strikeout pitchers get the big-money contracts; few fielders do. Indeed, one of the most disparaging remarks that can be made about an everyday player is "good-field, no-hit."[1] For two-thirds of a century fielding has been the most neglected aspect of baseball.

Defense deserves better. There's nothing more entertaining than a spectacular backhand stop by a shortstop, unless it's an over-the-fence catch by an outfielder, or a nifty scoop of a bad throw by a first baseman, or a slick throw in the pivot by a second baseman about to be clobbered by a sliding runner. Pitching and hitting don't offer the same thrills. Eventually one homer comes to resemble another, one strikeout the next, unless they occur in particularly dramatic situations. Ah, but defense is baseball's aesthetic keystone. Team highlight films are studded with spectacular fielding plays. Consider some of the greatest moments in World Series history: Willie Mays's catch in 1954, Sandy Amoros's catch in 1955, and Al Gionfriddo's in 1947, and particularly the glove work of Brooks Robinson in 1970. At one point Robinson raced to his right, caught a Lee

1. The term was coined in the 1930s by Cardinal scout Mike Gonzalez to describe Moe Berg, an infielder, catcher, World War II spy, and linguist. "He could speak eight languages," said former White Sox pitcher Ted Lyons, "but he couldn't hit in any of them."

May smash that was already behind his body, and threw him out while beyond the third-base line. "He was going toward the bullpen when he threw to first," Cincinnati reliever Clay Carroll recalled later. "His arm went one way, his body another, and his shoes another."

A team with good defense can always go higher in the standings. The great Baltimore clubs of the 1960s and 1970s were best known for their pitching and slugging. Equal billing belonged to perhaps the best left side of any infield—Robinson at third and Mark Belanger or Luis Aparicio at short. The pitchers induced ground balls, Brooks and Mark or Luis ate 'em up. "Good pitching isn't worth a damn without good fielding," says Ken (Hawk) Harrelson, the slugger-turned broadcaster-turned White Sox executive. John Felske, who became Philadelphia manager in 1985, underscores the importance of defense. "When you play poor defense, it has an effect on everything else, especially your pitching. When a pitcher has runners on first and second and gets that ground ball and we don't get to it—psychologically, that takes its effect. We're left wondering, 'Gee, what do I have to do to get out of this?' Or 'That should have been an easy double play and I should be winning, not losing.' Then only bad things happen, and I think last year, that's exactly what happened." Felske was speaking about 1984, when the Phillies committed 161 errors and finished fourth in the National League East. Alas, they made six in their first 1985 game and never contended for the division title.

The year 1985 was a model one for judging the importance of defense. Willie Wilson's spectacular catch of a Doug DeCinces fly helped give Kansas City the key victory over California in their battle for the AL West title. The Angels finished a strong second, partly because of their underrated infield of Rod Carew at first, Bobby Grich at second, Dick Schofield at short, and DeCinces at third; in all, the Angels turned 202 double plays, just 15 off the American League record. The Toronto Blue Jays won their first divisional title. Why? Among other things, because of their fine double play combination of second baseman Damaso Garcia and shortstop Tony Fernandez; their excellent outfield of George Bell in left, Lloyd Moseby in center, and Jesse Barfield in right spent the season throwing out speedsters like Wilson and Brett Butler. For their part, the Cardinals and Mets competed not only for the NL East, but for the honor of committing fewest errors in the National League. The Cards won both races. It's true that the Dodgers won the NL West title while leading the league in errors. Even so, three defensive moves helped propel them to the top: switching Mariano Duncan from the bench to shortstop, Dave Anderson from short to third (he was eventually succeeded there by Bill Madlock, a late-season acquisition from Pittsburgh), and Pedro Guerrero from third to left. Finally, the Royals and Cardinals set or tied some notable defensive records for a seven-game World Series: highest combined fielding average (.990), fewest errors by a team (two by St. Louis), fewest errors by two teams (five), most errorless games for a team (five by each), and most games played without errors by either team (four).

Normally we don't hear much about defensive records or statistics. There are no handy or catchy numbers like a .300 average or 20 wins. "They give pitchers saves," says utilityman Greg Pryor. "They ought to give fielders saves or game-winning catches or something like that." Until they do, fielders must settle for these decent but hardly decisive popular measures of fine defense:

Fielding percentage. Considered a good career stat, but it doesn't measure range. A nimble fielder reaching more balls than a slower man may commit more errors and have a lower percentage (the league leaders are sometimes slow-moving leftfielders with good gloves).

Total chances or assists per game. These numbers don't measure play under pressure and are much too relative. Sinkerball pitchers on grass will produce more grounders than high-ball pitchers on faster artificial turf.

Double plays. Pitching-poor teams tend to have high numbers because they put more men on base. "What counts," says St. Louis manager Whitey Herzog, "aren't the number of double plays but the ones you should have had and missed. You can't judge defense without a common denominator. You have to watch it every day."

But how do you judge defense on artificial turf? Now used in 10 of the 26 major league parks, it often makes fielding a batted ball either too hard or too easy. Because balls bounce high, outfielders risk having hits carom over their heads for inside-the-park homers; therefore, instead of charging in, they often choose to lay back. What's more, they're afraid to dive because they can't slide on hard carpets without risking turf burns. Many fly balls on turf fields bounce over walls for ground-rule doubles, robbing players and fans of close plays at second or third or home. In the infield some grounders bounce over fielders' heads.

The Wizard of Oz, St. Louis's great Ozzie Smith, in action. *Matthew L. Kaplan*

Others scoot so quickly that infielders can't flag them down—not even from their new and remote positions in the short outfield (the great play behind second is an endangered species). The accent is inordinately on arms rather than delicate glove work, where it belongs ("The first thing I look for in a shortstop is soft hands"—Ozzie Smith).

By contrast, balls hit directly to fielders on artificial turf are easier to catch than ever. Unless they kick off a seam in the carpet, most grounders take uniform hops. "On turf the ball comes to me and says, 'Catch me,'" explains Pryor. "On grass it says, 'Look out, sucker.'"

Those who want every bounce to be perfect and predictable should consider three of baseball's most delicious moments. In the eighth inning of the 1960 World Series finale, a potential double play ball took a bad bounce and struck Yankee shortstop Tony Kubek on the Adam's apple. The Pirates went on to score five runs in the inning and eventually won 10–9. In the seventh game of the 1924 Series, two bad-hop grounders bounced over the head of Giant third baseman Fred Lindstrom. The first drove in two runs and put the New York–Washington game into extra innings; the second produced the decisive run to end the Series. These moments of mirth and myth occurred on real grass and dirt. Some day most fields will be artificial, and most grounders will sit up like dull dogs.

Dave Concepcion of the Cincinnati Reds. *Cincinnati Reds*

Meanwhile, infielder and outfielder alike can't comfortably switch back and forth between dissimilar fields. "Concentration is especially important when you're switching from Astro-Turf to natural grass," says Philadelphia's Mike Schmidt, one of the best modern third basemen. "You can fail to get your glove down, look away, wait for the ball to come to you and still make the plays on AstroTurf because the bounce is usually uniform. I think AstroTurf causes defensive players to become lackadaisical. Then they switch to natural grass, where they have to charge the ball, and they're in trouble." Even as redoubtable a performer as Cincinnati shortstop Dave Concepcion suffers. In 1985 he committed 13 errors in 109 games on carpets, but 11 in 46 games on grass.

The greatest insult of all to fielding was the American League's adoption of the designated hitter in 1973. At every level of amateur and professional ball but the National League, the DH bats in place of the pitcher. That's all the guy does; he need not even own a glove! So all over America kids are growing up believing that they'll never have to learn to field well in order to make the majors. Their heroes are telling them in so many words that they're right. The first skill a major league outfielder often loses is his fielding ability. Reggie Jackson came to the Yankees in 1977 with the reputation of being a good rightfielder. He quickly became a defensive liability and was eventually switched to DH. Yet few took him to task for poor defense because, like most outfielders, he wasn't expected to work hard on his fielding. "Pitchers spend more time shagging flies than many outfielders," says former pitcher and pitching coach Jim Kaat.

A cherished baseball ritual being lost to designated hitters and artificial turfs is the sacrifice bunt. The player who most often lays down a sacrifice is the pitcher. In the National League, where he still bats, six of 12 parks have speedy artificial turf that makes precision bunting difficult. In all 14 AL parks, where the pitcher doesn't bat, his substitute, the DH, isn't expected to bunt often. What's lost is one of the most beautiful scenes in the game. As the hitter squares around, all nine fielders should be on the move. The catcher edges forward, preparing to charge onto the field. The pitcher and first and third basemen are moving toward the plate. The second baseman is covering first, and the shortstop is covering second. If they're doing their jobs, the rightfielder is backing up first, the centerfielder second, and the leftfielder third. All of it: threatened because of needless modern inventions.

Another less frequent but much more exciting play under attack is the suicide squeeze. Here's the typical squeeze situation in the National League: man on third, one out, number eight hitter up. He's usually a weak batter. If he's retired, the pitcher bats next, and in all likelihood the runner is as hopelessly stranded as a marooned sailor. Hence, the number eight man is given the squeeze signal. If he puts the ball in play, one of baseball's most exciting sequences—and exquisitely difficult fielding plays—follows. In the 1985 Series the DH wasn't used, and the squeeze was. "We only saw five or six squeezes all year," said Kansas City manager Dick Howser. "With the pitcher batting, you have to squeeze more." This too: vanishing because of the DH.

It's time defense made a comeback. Why not start with some barroom opinion and trivia? Who's the greatest defensive player at any one position? It would be hard to pass up shortstop Ozzie Smith (now with St. Louis), the best player at the toughest fielding position. All over baseball executives cringed in 1985 when the Cardinals gave Smith a $2.1-million-a-year contract. Not this corner. Smith's pact was long-overdue respect for his fielding. It's time glovemen everywhere trotted out that old slogan, "Millions for defense."

The most versatile defensive player? Why, good old Pete Rose![2] As Bill Deane noted in the March 1982 edition of *Baseball Digest*, Rose alone played more than 500 games and made the All-Star team at each of five positions (left, right, third, second, and first). He also led the league in fielding percentage at four positions (nobody else had ever led at more than two) and established the highest lifetime fielding percentage (.9911) of any outfielder in baseball history. Baseball experts properly rate Babe Ruth as the greatest player of all time because of his unique double achievement—beginning as one of baseball's most talented pitchers and finishing as its top slugger. Now it's time to take notice of Rose's hitting-and-fielding duo.

Author Deane further notes that only 12 players since 1900 have led their leagues in fielding percentage at each of two positions. The most recent was the Cardinals' Ken Oberkfell at second in 1979 and third in 1982 and 1983. In 1984 Yankee first baseman Don Mattingly became the ninth player to lead his league in hitting and fielding. The only father-son combo to win fielding titles are shortstops Dick Schofield, Sr. (1965) and Jr. (1984).

What's the toughest reserve job in baseball? Arguably that of a late-inning defensive replacement. "You have to go out there cold," says Bob Bailor, who played seven positions, "and you can't make up for your mistakes with your bat. Every error is magnified. They say pinch-hitting isn't easy; pinch-fielding may be tougher." Bailor motioned to his gloves—a small one he uses to play the middle-infield positions, a larger one for third base, and a larger one still for the outfield. "Before games I take grounders at three infield positions and then shag balls in the outfield. It's part of the job."

Sometimes playing a wholly unfamiliar position is part of the job. In 1985 Detroit infielder Tom Brookens, who had never caught, was inserted behind the plate for the final five innings of a 15-inning game. Only two runners stole on him, and the Tigers went on to win. "I never caught a game in my life," said Brookens. "It was fun." Manager Sparky Anderson underscored the importance of people like Brookens: "You can't win without them."

A good case in point is the Kansas City Royals, who have been in contention for titles steadily from the mid-'70s to the

---

2. Honus Wagner, who played half a dozen positions before settling at shortstop in his fifth full season, is a close second.

Pete Rose. *Cincinnati Reds*

mid-'80s. Sure, they've had fine leadership from people like George Brett and Hal McRae. Granted, they've had pitching, hitting, and speed. But let's not forget the versatile utility players who have helped their superb defenses: Pryor, John Wathan, Jamie Quirk, to name a few. Indeed, teammates always kid KC reliever Dan Quisenberry about being a "30-30-30" pitcher: 30 saves, 30 strikeouts, 30 great fielding plays to back him up.

What was the greatest fielding play of all time? Certainly, Smith's play on Burroughs in 1978 has to rank high. "Greatest fielding play I've ever seen because of the element of surprise he had to contend with," says baseball researcher Warner Fuselle. A similar play was made by Met second baseman Al Weis on June 4, 1969. With no score in the top of the fifteenth inning and a Dodger on third, Weis ran to his left for a hard grounder. The ball kicked to his right off the glove of pitcher Ron Taylor, whereupon Weis leaped back, grabbed the ball, and made an off-balance throw home to nip the runner. (The Mets scored to win the game in their half of the fifteenth.) On June 27, 1963, a Cleveland rightfielder named Al Luplow made a midair backhanded catch and tumbled over a five-foot fence into the right-field bullpen at Fenway Park to rob Boston's Dick Williams of a game-tying three-run homer. Making the catch was tough enough; executing a gymnastlike fall was even tougher. As he hurdled the fence with the ball in his glove, Luplow realized he was in for a rough landing. "If I'd kept going face first, I would have really hurt myself," he told *Sports Illustrated* contributor Jay Feldman years later. "I think my football background helped me because I tucked my left shoulder and rolled, and fortunately all I did was spike myself on the right knee."

What about catches far from major league diamonds? The best ever may have occurred at a Japanese game in 1981. Left-fielder Masafumi Yamamori of the Hankyu Braves actually climbed a fence and balanced himself on the wooden railing with his left foot and right hand while backhanding a drive by Sumio Hirota of the Lotte Orions. In 1983 Warner Fuselle conducted a survey for "This Week in Baseball" and questioned major leaguers about the greatest catch they'd ever seen. The majority picked "the Japanese catch." Pictures of the epic play reside in the Hall of Fame. As Casey Stengel used to say, you can look it up. Does that make Yamamori's catch the defensive play of the ages? Oh, no, and you'll have to read many a chapter to find out what is.

Are today's fielders better than yesterday's? The answer has to be: yes, because of improved gloves, more uniform surfaces, and bigger, stronger, faster, and better-coached athletes. In 1901 the American League fielding percentage was .938. In 1984 it was .979. Hall of Fame shortstop Rabbit Maranville committed 65 errors for the 1914 Miracle Braves; 70 years later Alan Trammell had 10 for the world champion Tigers.

But today's fielders shouldn't be satisfied with their play. In earlier times a major league second baseman might be the best fielder among 15 or 20 different second basemen in his organization. Chances are, he'd spent five or six years in the minors improving his skills. Most moderns advanced through today's depleted minor leagues in three or four years and probably skimped on their fielding. Understandably so, because pitching and power are all the rage today. Sluggers and slingers fill the parks, or so think team executives. "I negotiated 23 contracts with the Orioles," Brooks Robinson told the *Los Angeles Times*'s Bill Shirley, "and never once did a general manager say I had a great defensive year." Royal second baseman Frank White puts

Was this the greatest catch of all time? Leftfielder Masafumi Yamamori of the Hankyu Braves climbed a fence and balanced himself on the railing to steal a home run from the Lotte Orions' Sumio Hirota in 1981. *National Baseball Library*

it another way. "In a negotiating situation they'll tell you, 'If you shake a tree, you can always find a good glove.' But you can't always find good hands and feet to go with it." Yes, today's fielders are better than yesterday's. They'd be better still if they practiced fielding more and were better paid for it.

Happily, defense is starting to get its due. In recent years choice fielders Luis Aparicio, Pee Wee Reese, and Brooks Robinson were named to the Hall of Fame. "When they let me in," says Robinson, who carried a .267 lifetime average to Cooperstown, "they changed the rules."

2

Infield: Where the Action Is

The game will start in a few minutes. Most of the players are in the clubhouse, and most of the fans are focused on their hot dogs and beer. But there's a dance of beauty and grace and finesse and pace worth watching on the field. It's called infield practice, and it's being choreographed this particular day by a lanky Yankee third base coach named Gene (Stick) Michael.[1]

Michael bats a grounder, and his well-rehearsed students know just what to do with it. The shortstop throws it to the first baseman, who throws it to the catcher, who throws it to the second baseman, who throws it to first, who throws it home again: 6-3-2-4-3-2. Now Michael hits it to the second baseman, and the ball whips around again, this time in a sequence including the third baseman: 4-3-2-4-5-2. There are double play grounders to the four perimeter infielders and simulated bunts that the catcher throws to second and third. Finally, the infielders run back to the dugout, taking grounders and throwing home as they go: 5-2, 6-2, 4-2, 3-2. The exercise has been briskly conducted in a few minutes. Every player has known his role, and Michael has orchestrated the sequence perfectly. Bravo!

"It's a traditional loosening-up exercise," he says later. "You do it especially to stretch your arms and legs. The players who don't like it are usually people who can't throw, mainly catchers. The players who seem to like it most are guys who don't get to play very much. But everyone has to do it."

For good reason. The infield is where the action is. And the complexity. And the strategy. It's the heart and soul of defense.

"When you consider that 75 percent of the play is in the infield, you realize how much tougher it is to play there than outfield," says career third baseman Ron Cey. "You have to think

1. Michael became manager of the Cubs in 1986.

Gene "Stick" Michael. *National Baseball Library*

about covering the base, how hard the ball is going relative to the speed of the runner, if a grounder is likely to go to your left or right."

That's why much of the work has to be done before the ball is pitched. "We live and die by the charts," Houston manager Hal Lanier said when he coached the Cardinal infielders in 1982 (see profile at the end of this chapter). The Cardinals, among other teams, keep a record of every at-bat an opponent has had against their pitchers. Their charts include what kind of pitch was thrown, where it went in or out of the strike zone, where the batter hit it, and what the result was. The infielders are positioned and the batter is pitched according to past results.

Nonetheless, there are no guarantees of future results. "You can pitch a guy outside, and he'll still pull the ball," says Oriole coach Cal Ripken, Sr. "Don Baylor will do that. Sometimes we'll put a complete switch on him, with three men on the left side of the infield. Trouble is, he might get fooled or inside-out a pitch and hit it to right-center or down the right-field line. And Baylor will hit up the middle against a pitcher like Scott McGregor because he waits on changeups and breaking balls.

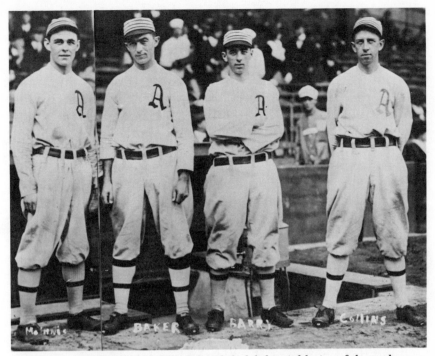

The famous "$100,000 Infield" of the Philadelphia Athletics of the early 1910s: Stuffy McInnis, Frank "Home Run" Baker, Jack Barry, and Eddie Collins. *National Baseball Library*

But the main thing you have to keep in mind is your pitcher, not the hitter. You find out how the pitcher's going in the first inning, and you react. If a pitcher's not in control, we'll play our fielders more straightaway; there's no telling where the balls will be hit, and there's more ground to cover away from the lines. We also allow our second baseman and shortstop to do some of their own positioning. Any time you're in the middle of the diamond, you can see how a batter is being pitched better than we can on the bench. I'll say this, though. We don't deviate from our set defense as much as we used to. That's because hitters don't choke up as much with two strikes and shorten their swings. It's become a long-ball game, and most guys keep swinging for the fences."

There are times when a fielder could be excused for throwing up his arms in despair. A middle infielder will have to shade toward second if he expects a runner like Rickey Henderson to steal. As a result, the batter can hit a grounder in the place the fielder has just vacated—yes, the hit-and-run. Clete Boyer, the former slick-fielding third baseman, told the *New Yorker*'s Roger Angell about an even more difficult situation. "'I still think the hardest play at third is when you've got a man on second who can steal a base and a left-handed batter up at the plate who can bunt. You've got to play up front on the grass and you know what they're thinkin'. My great example for that kind of trouble is Aparicio and Nellie Fox'—Luis Aparicio, the Hall of Fame shortstop with the White Sox and Orioles in the nineteen-fifties and sixties, and his stellar Chicago second base teammate, Nelson Fox. 'They could work that just perfect. If there's none out or one out, I've got to guess on each pitch if Luis is going to steal or if Nellie's up there to bunt. If I think Luis is stealing and he breaks, I got to get back and cover third, and then if Fox bunts the ball it's a base hit. If I break in two steps instead of one toward the plate, I can't get back—it's all over. Fans look at you playing back on the grass and grabbing that big line drive, but that play's routine, really. The other part is where the game is played.'"

Any knowledgeable baseball fan can name the most controversial aspect of positioning. It's deciding whether to play the first and third basemen close to the line late in a close game. Most managers guard the line religiously, arguing that a fielder there will prevent doubles into the corner. Tim McCarver, the broadcaster and former catcher, vehemently disagrees. "You see more games lost because guys guarded the line," he says. "Look at Jack Clark's single past George Brett in the ninth inning of the second 1985 Series game. If Brett hadn't been guarding the line, the ball would have been caught.[2] Instead, the Cardinals went on to score four runs and won the game. Most guys hit to the fat part of the field and up the gaps. As a hitter you have to use all parts of the field, or you're playing into the strength of the pitcher and catcher. That's why on defense you should place your fielders away from the lines; they'll be in a position to catch more balls."

Because of all the variables involved, some veteran infielders will almost always position themselves within the same few steps, theorizing that they might as well be where most balls are hit. No matter where he's positioned, though, the infielder has to be ready to change direction. "When the pitcher is wind-

2. KC manager Dick Howser replies: "We don't always play the line on pull hitters, but Clark's a dead pull hitter. If he pulls the ball down the line, it's a double at least. This way we still had a double play possibility. I won't second-guess myself on what happened. He reached out and raked a down-and-away pitch in the hole."

ing up, you see him out of your peripheral vision while you're watching the plate," says Michael, a former shortstop. "You know the pitch that's been called. If you're a middle infielder you may have relayed it to the third or first baseman. You know the pitcher's speed and habits—say, whether he changes speed on the breaking ball. As the ball's coming in, you watch the hitter's zone to see what he's likely to do with it. The way he's swinging will have you leaning; you can almost tell whether he'll hit it to your left or right. You can also be fooled. The pitcher won't always throw the ball where he wants to, and the hitter won't always swing the same way."

Nor will the fielder always field the same way. The traditionalists field grounders two-handed, but many of the middle infielders coming out of the Dominican Republic say they get down easier by using their glove hand alone. Nor is there unanimity about what to do once you've fielded the ball. With the Yankees leading the Brewers 3-2, men on first and third and no one out, second baseman Willie Randolph fielded a grounder hit right at him and surprised everyone by throwing home in time to nip Ted Simmons. The "book" play is to give up the run and go for the double play, especially since the throw from a middle infielder might be late. With as slow a runner as Simmons on third, however, Randolph took the gamble. It worked, and the Yankees went on to win 5-2. "A perfect example of an infielder thinking on his feet," a proud Michael said later.

But the most important plays infielders make are the instinctive ones. And the most important of the instinctive plays are double plays (which, admittedly, become instinctive only after considerable practice). Consider the pitchers who changed teams and became big winners—John Tudor of the 1985 Cardinals, to name one of the most recent. Did they suddenly get the hang of the slider, the perfect spin on the split-fingered fastball? Not likely. They probably got support for a change. Charles (Red) Barrett went from the Braves to the Cardinals in 1945; suddenly a 9-16 pitcher was 23-12. "I'm not doing anything differently," he said, "but [shortstop Marty] Marion and [second baseman Emil] Verban are. They're turning double plays." The DP is baseball's prime defense mechanism.

Infielders are constantly moving. On balls that are hit to the outfield with men in scoring position, the pitcher is backing up a base, and the first baseman is stationed at the mound to cut off the throw home. On a ball hit down the right-field line, the second baseman takes the relay, backed up by the first baseman. On a sure double down the left-field line, three different players—the shortstop, second baseman, and third baseman—may converge in the vicinity of third.

Teamwork is most visible in rundowns, when most of the infielders are bunched around one or another base. A well-drilled infield will rarely fail to tag out a runner caught in a rundown. The key words here are "well-drilled"; that's the only way to make this relatively sophisticated play look easy. "When you're chasing the runner, you hold the ball up and don't fake with it," says Michael. "By faking, you might fool the runner, but you could also fool the fielder you're throwing to. After you throw the ball, get out of the way; if you get in the runner's way, he can claim interference. But that's not where most of the mistakes are made. They're made either when you fake the fielder or don't run the runner hard enough. You always want to run the runner back to the lesser base, but the other day our catcher didn't run the guy hard enough back to third. Suddenly the third baseman had the ball, and he was running the guy toward the plate.[3] When the rundown is done best, the baseman without the ball is running toward the runner while the runner is running back toward him. The baseman gets the throw before the runner can change directions, and he's out." When the rundown is properly done, it looks like two cops collaring a bank robber; poorly done, the Keystone Kops.

Communication between fielders is very important. Calling for pop-ups is the most obvious and visible form of infield communication.[4] As most fans know, the second baseman and shortstop talk about covering the bag by conversing behind their gloves. In one popular system a fielder makes a closed-mouth signal when he wants to take the throw down, an open-mouthed signal when he wants his teammate to take it. Then there's what's commonly known as "infield chatter." In the Little Leagues, kids may be taught to support their pitchers with patter like "Hum, you chucka." In the big leagues they call that "false chatter." Most of the talk is technical. "George Brett is the only guy who will say anything personal to me," says Kan-

3. This happens altogether too often. In the sixth and final game of the 1917 World Series the White Sox beat the Giants 4–2; Chicago's three-run fourth inning included a rundown in which Eddie Collins was chased across the plate by third baseman Heinie Zimmerman.

4. The most famous communications lapse: the Red Sox were trailing the Giants 2–1 in the tenth inning of the 1912 Series finale when Tris Speaker's foul pop landed between catcher Chief Meyers and first baseman Fred Merkle. Given new life, Speaker singled in the tying run, and the Sox won the Series on Larry Gardner's sacrifice fly.

"Trio of bear cubs and fleeter than birds . . ." Joe Tinker and Johnny Evers, at bag; and, right, the Peerless Leader of the Chicago Cubs, Frank Chance.
National Baseball Library

sas City pitcher Bret Saberhagen. "He'll say something like, 'It's your game; don't let a reliever ruin it for you.' Bonesie [first baseman Steve Balboni] will tell me if he's playing behind the runner. Frank [second baseman Frank White] will come over to ask what signs we're using if there's a runner on second who could relay the signs we usually use to the batter. The shortstop will tell me who's covering second on a come-backer to me."

In the infield the manager can be as interesting a performer as the player. Let's think along with the skipper. Men on first and third, no one out, grounder to the third or first baseman. The runner on third breaks for home. "If it's slowly hit, go for home," says KC manager Dick Howser. "You probably wouldn't have time for a double play." Says Michael: "When the run is important, especially late in the game, you might go home. You might also go home if you're facing a tough pitcher or if you're having trouble scoring." In most situations managers will give up the run and get the double play to prevent the other team from having a big inning. That strategy especially holds when the ball's hit to a middle infielder playing back. Yes, like Randolph in the aforementioned example: the exceptions make the rule.

When do you bring the infield in? "Man on third, eighth or ninth inning, one man out," says Cardinal coach Red Schoendienst. "That's the most common situation. "You're not so close in with no one out because they won't run as often." In some early-game situations—facing a tough pitcher, needing to hold down the score because the team hasn't been hitting—managers will also bring the infield in. Just as they'll throw home with runners on first and third.

What to do when there are runners on first and second and the batter is sacrificing? In the usual sacrifice situation, with a man on first, three of the fielders move clockwise: shortstop covering second, second baseman covering first, first baseman charging in. With two runners on, some managers have begun using a weird maneuver called "the wheel play." In this situation the third baseman commits himself to fielding the bunt rather than covering the base. Meanwhile, the shortstop races the baserunner toward third on each pitch, the idea being to arrive ahead of him and take the throw for the force. It's a tough play best used by top infields.

Given the intricacy of infield defense, it's amazing how little innovative thinking there has been in recent years. Only a few major alignment changes are worthy of mention. When the pull-hitting Ted Williams was terrorizing pitchers in the 1940s, Cleveland manager Lou Boudreau placed three fielders to the right of second base. The Cardinals used the shift in the 1946 World Series, with second baseman Red Schoendienst fielding both grounders and sinking liners close to first baseman Stan Musial, and held Williams to five singles in seven games. In subsequent seasons Williams compensated by learning to hit occasionally to left. Later a reverse shift—three men to the left of second—was used against righthanded pull hitters. "When Hank Sauer was hitting, we'd shift so far over that I'd be playing in the shortstop hole," says Schoendienst, a second baseman. In some emergency situations—say, bases loaded, no one out in the ninth inning of a tie game—Gene Mauch and a few other managers have used five infielders and two outfielders. Dick Williams sometimes has his second baseman charge the plate on obvious bunt situations. And that's about it: all the ingenuity, all the intuition, all the creativity the feeble and fearful mind of the baseball manager has mustered these many years.

Further innovations are long overdue. Herewith some suggestions:

Against extreme righthanded pull hitters, bring back some Branch Rickey stratagems. Move the second baseman to short and the shortstop to short left-center. That's where the shortstop began back in the 1840s: as a short-fielder somewhere beyond second base. Another possibility: use the shortstop in straightaway left-center, creating four deep-fielders. With left-handed pull hitters, leave the second baseman where he is and put the shortstop in right-center.

There's a rule stating that only the catcher may be positioned in foul territory. Repeal it. When Dwight Gooden is facing some stiff he's struck out the last 12 times, everyone but the pitcher and catcher should leave the field for toast and tea in the dugout. Satchel Paige used this ploy when he was barnstorming. If the stuffy rulesmakers balk, bring in the outfield and have nine infielders. Dizzy Dean did it; why not Doc Gooden?

Conversely, when a hitter like Wade Boggs is up looking for some hole in the outfield, put everyone out there but the pitcher, catcher, and first baseman. If the sucker wants to bunt, let him try.

The optimum team effort is the triple play. There have been dozens of them in baseball history, only eight of which were unassisted.[5] The optimum situation for the triple play: men on first and second, grounder near the third-base bag. The third baseman steps on third for the force and fires around the horn for outs at second and first. Brooks Robinson, one of the slowest players ever, hit into four triple plays. Brooks Robinson, one of the best third basemen ever, started three triple plays in the field.

There has been every variety of double play, too, like the twin killing that starts with a backhand stop in the hole by the shortstop, continues with a nifty pivot by the second baseman, and concludes with a fine stretch by the first baseman. "The poet or storyteller who feels that he is competing with a superb double play in the World Series is a lost man," said the late novelist and short-story writer John Cheever. "One would not want as a reader a man who did not appreciate the finesse of a

5. On June 30, 1968, Washington shortstop Ron Hansen made the last unassisted triple play in baseball history, before 5,937 fans in Cleveland. The Indians won anyway, 10–1, and Hansen, who also had an error and four strikeouts, was traded to the White Sox two days later.

double play." The DP Cheever must have appreciated best was the one that ended the 1921 World Series. The Giants were leading the Yankees 1-0 with Aaron Ward on first and one out in the ninth inning, when the Yankees' Frank Baker hit what looked like a sure single. Shortstop Johnny Rawlings made a superb stop and threw to first baseman George Kelly for the out. Let Kelly describe what happened next: "Ward was half-way to third when I turned the ball loose to [Frankie] Frisch. It was a perfect throw and beat Ward by about half a second to complete the double play and end the game and Series." The play goes 6-3-5 if you're scoring.

More spectacular still was a single out involving three players on September 8, 1947. In the seventh inning of a Cleveland–New York game at Yankee Stadium, the Yanks' Bill Johnson hit a hard grounder in the hole. Cleveland third baseman Ken Keltner just missed it, but shortstop Lou Boudreau backhanded it. Before tumbling head over heels toward the line, Boudreau blindly flipped the ball behind his back to Keltner, who fired to first baseman Les Fleming just ahead of Johnson: 6-5-3 if you're scoring. "[Coach] Bill McKechnie had tears in his eyes when he returned to the dugout," Boudreau said later. "He said it was the first time he had seen that play in 46 years in baseball." Boudreau and Keltner had practiced it in spring training.

When he was a second baseman in the minors, Gene Mauch fielded a ball behind second. Out of position to make a sure throw to first, he shoveled the ball to his shortstop, who made the relay as if it had been a double play: 4-6-3. Giant second baseman Duane Kuiper and shortstop Johnnie LeMaster worked the same play on August 1, 1983. The Yankees used a multiplayer putout on balls hit to the right of first baseman Jim Spencer. The lefthanded Spencer would field the ball and throw it to Randolph, who then fired to the pitcher covering first: 3-4-1.

Today's infielders are better than ever. For one thing, they're trained by a modern invention called infield coaches. "I had more coaching in high school than after I turned pro," says former Pirate second baseman Bill Mazeroski, whose career ended in 1972. By contrast, contemporary infielders dance that infield dance before every game. "The kids in the stands like to watch it," says Michael. "They're in awe. How can the players make it look so easy, so accurate?"

OBERKFELL, SMITH, HERR, AND HERNANDEZ

They're not as celebrated as the best-known infields, like the Yankee and Dodger foursomes of the 1950s, the Reds of the mid-1970s, the Tinker-to-Evers-to-Chance[6] double play combination, and Connie Mack's $100,000 infield of Stuffy McInnis at first, Eddie Collins at second, Jack Barry at short, and Frank (Home Run) Baker at third. Even so, the Cardinals of 1982 were probably the best (if most short-lived) defensive infield of all time. Remember these names, schoolchildren: Ken Oberkfell at third, Ozzie Smith at short, Tommy Herr at second, Keith Hernandez at first.

Any infield with Smith and Hernandez—arguably the best ever at their positions—is bound to be respectable. Their teammates played almost as well. Oberkfell led all National League third basemen with a .972 fielding percentage, and Herr made only nine errors. Together the foursome and their estimable sub, Mike Ramsey, averaged only 10.6 errors apiece. No wonder the Cardinals led the league in fielding percentage (.981) and chances (6,558) and were second in double plays (169).

Manager Whitey Herzog created this monster. In 1981 he switched Oberkfell from second to third, replacing good-hands, no-range Ken Reitz. The Cardinals immediately ran up the best record in the division but won neither half-title in that strike-shortened season. Next, Herzog cast about for a replacement for his unhappy shortstop, Garry Templeton. And lo, he found that the best shortstop in the game, San Diego's Ozzie Smith, was available. The result was St. Louis's first world championship since 1967.[7]

All the Cardinal infielders had good hands—the prime requisite—and were equally sound on turf or grass. Ramsey, Oberkfell, and Herr were signed as shortstops, the infield's most difficult position, and began working out at other spots when Templeton looked as if he'd be a fixture at short. Herr and Hernandez were high school quarterbacks. Hence, Herr's toughness in the pivot and Hernandez's strong arm.

The Cardinal infielders communicated much more than most. Theirs was more than the routine "I'll take the throw down" patter. "Ozzie! Obie!" Hernandez called out when he was play-

6. That's Joe Tinker at short, Johnny Evers at second, and Frank Chance at first. Their third baseman, trivia buffs, was Harry Steinfeldt.
7. Unfortunately, Herzog began dismantling the infield by trading Hernandez in June 1983.

Arguably the finest of infields of all time, the 1982 World Champion
St. Louis Cardinals: clockwise, Ken Oberkfell, Ozzie Smith, Tommy Herr,
and Keith Hernandez. *St. Louis Cardinals*

ing far off the line against a righthanded pull hitter. He was telling them to delay the throw until he reached first. Herr gave a verbal signal to Hernandez, who couldn't see the catcher's sign from his spot at first, when a righthanded pitcher was about to throw a breaking ball to a lefthanded batter; that way Hernandez knew he should shade to the line. Smith sometimes, but not as often, told Oberkfell when a lefty pitcher was throwing slow stuff to a righthanded batter. "A lot of the time I'll tell him I don't want to know," Oberkfell said. "If it's a fastball, you have a tendency to relax. I want to be ready all the time." With two outs and a man on first Oberkfell would tell Herr to expect a throw to second on a grounder. Any time one player shifted position, the others did too. "We don't want to leave too many holes," said Oberkfell.

They weren't exactly Swiss cheese.

3

Pitcher: Getting Around
the Mound

Several members of the Texas Ranger pitching staff were sitting in the clubhouse one afternoon in 1985 discussing the importance of fielding. They were quick to agree with Los Angeles manager Tommy Lasorda's assertion that a good-fielding pitcher can help himself win another two games a year. "It's really very simple," said Burt Hooton. "It's a question of a pitcher's very function: not putting too many runners on base."

"As soon as you release the ball," put in Dave Schmidt, "you're a fielder."

"When Ed Halicki was with the Giants," said Charlie Hough, "he was told he'd be sent down after his next start. Then he found himself protecting a one-run lead in the ninth. Somebody hit a liner at him, and he barehanded it and threw to first for a double play. He went on to win the game. He wasn't sent down."

"Fernando Valenzuela is the best I've ever seen at fielding grounders hit right at him," said Hooton. "Unlike most of us, he gets his glove all the way down. He's not as great at covering first."

"But that's the most important thing a pitcher can do on defense!" said Dave Rozema.

Yes it is. Hence, the critical and evocative drill that starts every spring training. The play is the very essence of spring: grounder to first, pitcher covering. It's as simple as three to one.

"It's gathering time, like a class reunion," says former major league pitcher Jim Kaat (see profile at the end of this chapter). "All of a sudden, you're in the home room, with 19 or 20 pitchers talking about what happened during the winter."

And working on the 3-1 play. It's a drill pitchers practice before they work a single game, a play they repeat until they see it in their dreams. That's because Lasorda and the Rangers were right about pitchers winning games with their gloves, and there's probably no play they make more often than the 3-1 putout.

The drill takes longer than any other because of the number of players involved. All the pitchers—veterans, rookies, minor leaguers up for a quick look—participate, along with three or four first basemen. A weathered coach bats out grounders.

"It's a more difficult drill for the pitcher than for us first basemen," says Chris Chambliss, who starred for the Indians, Yankees, and Braves, "because none of them run it as often as each of us does. They're not as accustomed to the play. Besides, during the game they're thinking of getting the batter out, and I'm thinking of playing defense."

Games can turn on how fast a pitcher reacts. "I learned to break for first on any ball hit to the right side of the infield," says Kaat, who won more Gold Gloves (16) than any other pitcher. "When a hitter beats a pitcher, nine times out of 10 it's because the pitcher didn't get a jump." Kaat used to head for a spot 10 to 15 feet down the line from first base. Then he'd turn sharply left and race parallel to the line. If all went well, he'd catch the first baseman's toss a couple of steps ahead of the base. Then he'd look for the base and touch it with his right foot to avoid colliding with the runner. "If you practice it enough," says Kaat, "you'll get your footwork down like a hurdler."

Of course, the play is not as simple as the neat 3-1 on our scorecard. For one thing, the throw doesn't always go from first baseman to pitcher. A bunt or slowly topped grounder can be fielded by either player. (If both converge on the ball, the second baseman should cover first, but for some reason, he rarely participates in the spring training drill.) Also, the first baseman's throw to the pitcher may not be perfect. "I look for bad throws because I know I can handle the good ones," says Phil Niekro of the Braves, Yankees, and Indians. Niekro also doesn't panic about tagging the bag. Pitchers usually err when they look for the base before they have the ball.

The play looks simple enough when the ball is hit sharply to the first baseman, who then flips an underhand throw, chest-high, to the pitcher a couple of steps before he reaches the bag. Things start getting complicated, both in practice and games, when a ball is hit any distance to a first baseman's right. An underhand toss won't get the job done in such instances; the throw must then be sidearm or overhand and may not be right on the money.

A 3-1 play figured in the most exciting Series finale ever played. The Yankees were leading the Pirates 7-5 in the eighth inning of the 1960 Series' seventh game, with Pittsburgh runners on second and third and two outs. When Roberto Clemente hit a chopper to the right of first baseman Moose Skowron, a standard 3-1 play should have ended the inning. Unfortunately for the Yankees, Bobby Shantz, the best-fielding pitcher of his time, had been replaced by the sluggish Jim Coates. When Coates was slow covering first, Clemente was safe, a run scored, and the stage was set for a three-run homer by Hal Smith. The Pirates eventually won 10-9. Yankee fans are still fuming over manager Casey Stengel's decision to replace Shantz with Coates.

A 3-1 play was the most critical in the 1985 World Series. With the Cardinals three outs away from taking the Series in six games, St. Louis pitcher Todd Worrell caught a throw from first baseman Jack Clark and stepped on first for what looked like a close but certain 3-1. Umpire Don Denkinger, however, called batter Jorge Orta safe, and the Royals rallied to win the game. They took the Series the following night.

Fielding would be tough enough for a pitcher if the 3-1 play were all he had to make. It's not. The pitcher has to break to his left fast enough to cut off a drag bunt down the first base line; if the ball gets by him, it's invariably a hit. Sometimes the 3-1 play doesn't occur because the first baseman doesn't get to a slowly hit ball in the hole. The second baseman does, and the play goes to the pitcher: 4-1. Another corollary to the 3-1 play is the 3-6-1 double play. The first baseman fields a ball in the hole and throws to the shortstop covering second. With the first baseman out of the play, the shortstop then relays to the pitcher covering first. In this case, the pitcher somehow catches the ball as he's looking over his left shoulder. Then he has to find the bag. Strange things can happen. On May 24, 1985, Charlie Hough induced Boston's Rich Gedman to hit a double play ball with the Rangers leading the Red Sox by one run in the ninth, one out, and men on first and third. Gedman hit a one-hopper to first baseman Pete O'Brien, who threw to shortstop Curtis Wilkerson covering second. Then Wilkerson relayed to first. Hough caught the ball, stepped on first to end the game—and tripped over the bag.

Most of the time a pitcher's fielding is no laughing matter.

There's often a direct correlation between good fielders and big winners. Consider some of the most respected fielders to pitch in the last 10 years. Tom Seaver. Jim Kaat. Fernando Valenzuela. Phil Niekro. Ron Guidry. By no coincidence, all of them may be Hall of Fame candidates.

Here's what a pitcher can do to help his team win a game. On June 29, 1974, the Cubs were leading the Expos 2-1 in the ninth, with Montreal runners on first and third and one out, when Ron Hunt tried to lay down a suicide squeeze bunt. He popped it up along the first-base line, and Cub pitcher Rick Reuschel dived for the ball and caught it just a few inches off the ground. Then he threw to first to double up a runner and end the game.

Here's what a pitcher can do to win a big game. In the fifth game of the 1964 World Series, the Cardinals' Bob Gibson, a righthander who always twisted toward the first-base line on his follow-through, was hit on the buttock by a liner off the bat of the Yankees' Joe Pepitone. The ball caromed over to the third-base line. After spinning around Michael Jackson style, Gibson ran down the ball, retrieved it, and threw out Pepitone in what became the game's pivotal play. "It didn't seem like much at the time, but I still don't know how I did it," says Gibson. Other pitchers often contribute to losses by dropping throws from their first basemen. That's what happened to the Cardinals' Dave LaPoint in the 1982 World Series. LaPoint isn't a great athlete. The agile Gibson went to Creighton University on a basketball scholarship.

The only play a pitcher is likely to make as often as the 3-1 putout is the throw to first, second, or occasionally third in a bunt situation. It's a play that doesn't come easily. After all, the pitcher is accustomed to being totally in charge before throwing the ball. Look at him out there: standing on the rubber, taking a deep breath, assuming the proper grip, throwing when ready. Suddenly, the ball's in play and he must field it, turn, sight the base, and throw quickly—all without getting a good grip on the ball. Often his throw is hurried. Often it's off. In one of baseball's strangest ironies, the man who holds the ball and initiates the action often comes unglued.

"On a bunt situation the most important thing is the first three steps," says Kaat. "Coming off the mound, the pitcher should take three strong strides. The closer he gets to the ball, the smaller his strides should be, so that he can get his body under control. While listening to his catcher tell him which base to throw to, he should get his hand up to the throwing position as quickly as possible. That way the fielder he's throwing to can see the ball, and the pitcher can make a better throw. Finally, he should spin off his back foot and take a little crow-hop before throwing. That gets his body under control and his momentum going toward the base."

There are other defensive jobs a pitcher must familiarize himself with. Like backing up third or home if a play is being made there. The idea is not to stand near the catcher or third baseman, but near the fence; that way, a pitcher can reach overthrows that kick to the side as well as those that go through the fielder.

Holding runners on base is another defensive skill the pitcher must master. Actually, the term "pickoff" is misunderstood. The idea isn't as much to pick off a runner as it is to keep him close to the base. To put it another way, a pitcher who picks off five runners a season but allows 30 to steal may not be as valuable as a pitcher who picks off two or three but allows none to steal.[1] White Sox great Wilbur Wood would throw to first so many times the runner would be lulled to sleep. Most often the key ingredient isn't the throw to first as much as the quick pitch home. The pitchers who do this best are those who don't waste time. They come to the "stop" position on their windup with their weight on their back foot, so they won't have to rock back before throwing. And they minimize the leg kick and throwing motion. A quick delivery invariably follows. A pitch that reaches the plate in 1.3 seconds or less won't yield many stolen bases because the average catcher can get the ball to second in 2.0. The total of 3.3 is quicker than most baserunners with a lead can race from first to second.

Finally, there's the business of handling grounders like any other infielder. Hall of Famer Whitey Ford was so adept at fielding up-the-middle balls that his shortstop and second baseman could play unusually wide of the bag. By doing so, Ford affected the entire Yankee infield. Harvey Haddix was the same way. Tom Seaver used to take 30 minutes of fielding practice, working not only on catching the ball but making the tough turnaround throw to second. The most difficult fielding play a pitcher makes on grounders is the high bouncer hit over his head. Bob Gibson made one of these back-to-the-plate plays,

1. Not that a pickoff can't be useful. The Orioles were once forced to use a reserve infielder, Lenn Sakata, as their tenth-inning catcher. Three Toronto players reached first. None stole second, or even tried to. Tippy Martinez picked off each one.

The Yankees' Whitey Ford, whose fielding skills as a pitcher made him a "fifth infielder" for the Bronx Bombers. *New York Yankees*

turned almost all the way round in midair, and threw a basketball chest pass to first. Hall of Fame pitcher Dizzy Dean called it the best fielding play he ever saw. "You have to think about the ball being hit to you, want it to be," says White Sox scout Bart Johnson, a former big-league pitcher. "Then you have to know what to do with it. Look at how well trained the Detroit and Baltimore pitchers are; after they've fielded the ball, they get rid of it as quickly as anyone."

All of which is mere prelude to the real blood and guts of fielding the pitching position: staying alive. Johnson describes the starkness of it all. "We pitchers always get a kick out of third base being described as the hot corner," he says. "Hot corner? If the third baseman crept in 50 feet from home plate, people would say, 'He's nuts: He'll get harelip.' We pitchers are 50 feet from home every time we follow through!"

Every pitcher has been hit on some part of his anatomy by a

line drive or hard-hit ground ball. Most escape without serious injury.[2] All live in fear of experiencing the same fate as Cleveland's Herb Score. Once boasting a fastball reminiscent of Bob Feller's, Score was hit in the face in 1957 by a line drive off the bat of the Yankees' Gil McDougald. Score was never the same again. Nor was the White Sox' Wood after his kneecap was shattered by a Ron LeFlore liner in 1976.

Describing a Wade Boggs liner hit to the mound, Kansas City reliever Dan Quisenberry said, "It played pinball wizard on my legs. He lit up all the bonus lights, plus a free game." Quisenberry escaped unharmed, but considerably more philosophical about his chosen profession. "My ambition is never to be on the disabled list. I don't want to be hit by any more line drives. It's not fair. We're too close, and they can hit it harder than we can throw it."

Pitchers have their best and worst moments contending with these shots. Before fielding Luis Salazar's sharp one-hopper early in 1985, Yankee reliever Dave Righetti made a 180-degree turn on his follow-through. Then he caught the ball between his legs. "All that was," Righetti said truthfully, "was protecting myself." Even more memorable was a play Gibson made in which a line drive by Roberto Clemente shattered his leg. Gibson picked up the ball and threw out the runner. Then Gibson was carried to the hospital. Talk about profiles in courage.

For years there's been a lively debate about how a pitcher should prepare for those hard-hit balls. "You show me a pitcher following through in good fielding position and I'll show you a pitcher who ain't following through," said Dizzy Dean. Actually, there have been some pitchers like Seaver who naturally finish the delivery square to the hitter and glove held high. "It's a delicate balance," says Kaat. "You don't want to alter a pitcher's motion to the point where he isn't throwing his best stuff, but you do want him to protect himself." For his part, Kaat resisted the temptation to wear a huge glove. He might have better protected his face that way, but he probably would have restricted his mobility. Kaat wore a small but supple mitt and took his chances.

The bottom line is that every pitcher can protect himself only so much in the face of 150-mph liners. He needs some luck too. That's why pitchers think less about the hospital bill and

2. Including, incredibly, George Brunet, who pitched for 35 years without a jockstrap.

more about the 3-1 drill. It's straightforward. It's sociable. And it's safe.

JIM KAAT

In 1959 a big 20-year-old kid out of Michigan named James Lee Kaat ambled onto a major league field for the first time, wearing the uniform of the Washington Senators. In 1983 a 44-year-old Jim Kaat played his last major league game, for the St. Louis Cardinals. In between he made an excellent case for selection to the Hall of Fame. Kaat had pitched an unprecedented 25 years over four decades in the big leagues, won 283 games, helped to popularize the quick-pitch delivery, and revolutionized training methods by continuing to throw between starts. Kaat will be equally well remembered for his fielding. He won 16 Gold Gloves—more than any other pitcher. He could make all the plays in the field, and he could explain how to do them too. That's why he went on to coach the Cincinnati Reds pitching staff in 1985.

"A pitcher's got to be aware that almost every time the ball is hit, there's someplace he's got to be other than the mound," says Kaat, who is now in broadcasting. "Ball hit to the right side: cover first. A single: back up the second baseman so that the first baseman can stay on the bag and prevent the runner from taking liberties. Base hit with a man on first: back up third. Base hit with a man in scoring position: back up the plate."

Among the greatest-fielding pitchers of all time you can make an equally strong case for either Bob Gibson or Jim Kaat. Gibson is celebrated for spectacular plays; Kaat prided himself on perfecting the more routine but also more frequent plays. No one made the 3-1 putout better. No one moved faster to his right coming off the mound. And certainly no one thought more intelligently about fielding. Asked which play he remembers most fondly, Kaat cites the three 3-1 plays he and Minnesota first baseman Harmon Killebrew made on the Dodgers' speedy Willie Davis in a 1965 World Series game. He's also proud of the many grounders that he turned into double plays.

Not that Kaat couldn't make spectacular plays too. He once raced over to the dugout to make a sensational grab of a foul ball his catcher had lost sight of. And a memorable series of events brought Kaat's fielding to the world's attention in the first place.

Nobody, but nobody, was better at making the 3-1 play, first to pitcher, than the veteran Jim Kaat, here shown taking the throw at first base. *Matthew L. Kaplan*

"There was a game in 1962 when I was hit in the mouth by a high-bouncing grounder," he says. "The play cost me six teeth. The next time I pitched, two ground balls were hit back to me—sharp one-hoppers—and I got them both. People took note." He won the first of his 16 consecutive Gold Gloves that year.

Like most of the good-fielding pitchers, Kaat was an excellent athlete. "Growing up, I was always one of the smaller kids, and I had quick reflexes and good coordination," says Kaat, who has excelled in basketball, golf, and handball as well as baseball. "When I reached my full height (6′5″), I still had these qualities." Of equal importance, Kaat has an agile mind. Long before it was fashionable, he was giving up red meat and stressing strength, flexibility, and stretching exercises in his training. While other pitchers were haphazard in their fielding practice, Kaat rehearsed every play he'd have to make until it became second nature. And as a coach he made sure his pitchers did likewise. "We had a drill," he says, "in which pitchers used a cloth-covered 'Incrediball.' They hit it at each other as hard as they could from 50 feet. It sharpened their reflexes."

It's obvious that Kaat's influence on fielding will be felt long after the end of his playing career.

4

Catcher: The Tools of Intelligence

What a way to go: Toronto catcher Buck Martinez was lost for the remainder of the 1985 season when he broke his right fibula and dislocated his right ankle while making a weird and heroic double putout in a July 9 game at Seattle. The play began with rightfielder Jesse Barfield throwing to Martinez in an effort to nip Phil Bradley, who was trying to score from second on Gorman Thomas's single. Bradley ran hard into Martinez. Dazed, lying on his back, Martinez nonetheless held onto the ball for the out. Then he saw Thomas heading for third, and, half rising, threw there. The ball sailed wide of the base, whereupon Thomas headed home, and leftfielder George Bell headed after the throw. Still writhing, Martinez caught Bell's peg on a short hop and tagged out Thomas. A few other catchers have tagged two runners on the same play. Not many were subsequently carried off the field on a stretcher.

What a way *not* to go: In the twelfth inning of the 1970 All-Star Game, Cleveland catcher Ray Fosse suffered a badly separated shoulder when Cincinnati's Pete Rose crashed into him for the winning run. Fosse, who had 16 homers at the time, hit only two more that season and never again topped 12. "The shoulder became so inflamed that it masked the break and separation on the X-ray," said Fosse. "They didn't even know it was broken until the following spring. But I kept playing. You had to look like you were hurt in order to come out of the lineup. I took painkillers and kept playing until I broke my finger September 1. I didn't want people to think I was faking it."

How easy it is to overlook the one daily reality of a catcher's life that Martinez and Fosse knew only too well: pain. Constant pain. Interminable pain. And pain, unfortunately, that the catcher is expected to endure quietly. His job is not to be healthy. He's viewed first and foremost as the pitcher's best friend—a kind of combination shrink, soothsayer, and surrogate father. The pain just comes with the territory.

No exercise therapist worth his jump rope would recommend deep knee bends for good health, but the catcher does hundreds of them a week. When Cincinnati's Johnny Bench (see profile at end of chapter) decided to reduce his catching load to two games a week, *Sports Illustrated*'s Steve Wulf estimated that Bench had already done 335,200 deep knee bends over 13 seasons. And paid for it, not only with bad knees but with everything else a man has to endure from being grotesquely bent over for some 3,000 hours: four broken bones in his feet, two in his hands, lower-back spasms, circulation trouble in his hands, scars from surgery on his left shoulder, and gnarled toenails.

If the poor catcher isn't pained enough from squatting there, he's constantly taking physical and existential lumps from home plate collisions, foul tips, and a host of other, less obvious torments. In 1976 a splinter from a bat lodged in the neck of former Dodger catcher Steve Yeager, nearly killing him. Now many catchers have pieces of metal that look like shoehorns hanging from their masks to guard what had been one of their few unprotected body parts. Even the simple peg to second can be tortuous. "It's the toughest throw in baseball," says Cub catcher Jody Davis. "You have to get rid of it quickly, throw it hard, and be accurate. Stiffness sets in because you're constantly trying to throw from an awkward position."

One of the most dizzying sights in baseball is that of a catcher eyeing a foul pop. Holding his mask in his hand, he looks skyward. The ball is somewhere overhead, curving he knows not where. He tries to get a bead on it. He staggers under it, hoping he doesn't crash into the fence or screen. He discards his mask, reaches for the ball, and . . . In one of the most famous sequences of the decade Bob Boone of the Phillies reached for a foul pop representing the penultimate out of the 1980 World Series. It bounced out of his glove—right into the mitt of ever-alert first baseman Pete Rose. Boone was lucky. So was Yogi Berra. When Yogi dropped a Ted Williams foul that would have completed Allie Reynolds's pennant-clinching no-hitter in 1951, Williams hit another pop that Yogi caught. Hank Gowdy wasn't so lucky. The Giant catcher tripped on his mask and dropped a

Yogi Berra missing Ted Williams's high foul and endangering Allie Reynold's pennant-clinching no-hitter in 1951. Williams then hit another foul, which Berra took to clinch the game and the championship for the New York Yankees. *Sporting News*

foul pop, contributing to the Senators' Series-winning inning in 1924. But mostly the problem is just getting to the ball. "When the ball comes off the bat on a pop-up to the catcher, it's going to come back to you," says the Mets' Gary Carter. "You're always backing up. So what I try to do is back up right away. That way I'm walking into the ball, which is much easier."

There are only so many foul pops per game for a catcher to catch. More frightening are the high pitches, low pitches, inside and outside pitches that come his way each inning. Every catcher knows the sad tale of Mickey Owen, the Dodger catcher who allowed a pivotal passed ball in the 1941 World Series. Owen dropped Hugh Casey's sweeping low curve for what should have been the swinging strike three that evened the Yankee-Dodger Series at two games apiece.[1] Instead, the batter, Tommy Henrich, reached base, the Yankees went on to win, and New York wrapped up the Series the next day. Perhaps as

1. According to those who were in a position to know, it was a spitball—which was why it broke off so sharply.

New York Mets

Kansas City Royals

Kansas City's Jim Sundberg, top right; the New York Mets' Gary Carter, top left; and the White Sox' Carlton Fisk crouched behind the plate with George Brett batting. *Matthew L. Kaplan*

a result, catchers have a kind of gallows humor about tough pitches. "The key thing about blocking pitches in the dirt isn't so much getting the body in front of the ball," Carter said before the 1983 All-Star Game. "It's having no fear. Take a look." He removed his jersey and exposed a chest covered with bruises. "It's fun blocking balls." He winked at Atlanta's Bruce Benedict. "Right, Benny?"

"Instinct after a while," said Benedict.

"Just let it hit you," said Carter.

No one gets as banged up as often as a major league catcher. One day Kansas City's Jim Sundberg began touching his body parts like a third-base coach going through signals to a hitter. "I took a couple of foul tips on my shoulder," he said. "I hurt my hand in a collision at the plate. I don't know what I did to my ankle, but it hurt for a while too." He didn't mention that he was disabled at the time with taped ribs, having pulled a muscle in his left rib cage during batting practice. The catcher with the low pain threshold moves quickly to another position.

"In the past, catchers wouldn't condition themselves in the off-season," says Sundberg. "What we've learned is that you not only have to condition yourself in the off-season, but during the

The Pittsburgh Pirates' Tony Pena takes a pitch, prepares to throw to third, then races to take part in a run-down against the Houston Astros. Denny Walling is the batter. *Matthew L. Kaplan*

season." The most notable new fitness buff is the White Sox' Carlton Fisk, who does every manner of stretching exercise in-season and out and spends as much time in the weight room as a bodybuilder. The most athletic of all big-league catchers may be Tony Pena, who presents the lowest target to a pitcher and has the most mobility coming out of the crouch. The swiftest catcher is former KC receiver John Wathan, who stole 36 bases in 1982, an unofficial record for his position.

The corollary to a catcher's pain is his fatigue. The player who seems to handle it best is Boone, who moved from Phila-delphia to California at age 34 in 1982 and hopes to play the position well into his forties and set a career record for games caught. "Being tired is in the head," says Boone. "If you start to think, 'Gee, I'm tired, I must be losing something,' you're dead. The way I see it, I may be tired, but there's something in re-serve. I learned a long time ago not to assess myself. That's someone else's job. They'll have to tell me I can't play because I have a broken neck. I look at catching the same as any other position. If it's tougher, condition yourself better."

Boone takes a sterner view of his position than others do. He has no choice. "Some guys like Fisk could DH or play first, third, or left because of their bats," he says. "I never hit well enough to do anything but catch. Besides, I was a third base-man in the Phillie organization when Mike Schmidt was com-ing up."

Like many of his peers, Boone realized that the quickest route to the majors was catching, which is far and away the most unpopular position among youngsters. Boone saw a bright side. In return for enduring all manner of injury while some-how making big winners of average pitchers, he wouldn't have to hit well. How useful can a weak-hitting catcher be? Bill James had a telling observation in his annual *Baseball Abstract*. In 1984 the Angels' earned run average was 3.79 when Boone caught, 4.75 when he didn't. It mattered not that he hit .202. "As far as I'm concerned, the only responsibility a catcher has is to control his pitchers," says Detroit manager Sparky Ander-son, who has had two of the best catchers in Cincinnati's Bench and the Tigers' Lance Parrish. "He doesn't have to get a hit as long as he can do that."

One of the primary functions of a catcher is to encourage a pitcher to throw pitches he's afraid of. Said former California pitching coach Tom Morgan, "Boonie has guys throw pitches they wouldn't have in the past—say, a changeup on 2-1 or a

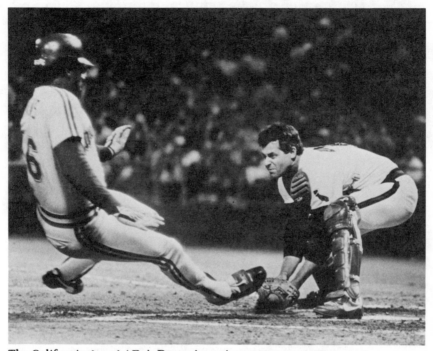

The California Angels' Bob Boone in action. *V.J. Lovero, California Angels*

slider on 3-1—and that gives them more confidence. Basically, that's all pitching is—confidence." A case in point was Don Aase. "Earlier in the season I threw a couple of pitches in the dirt that got by Boonie for wild pitches," he said in 1982. "Later he came to me and said, 'I know how your curve breaks; that won't happen again.' So I wasn't afraid to keep throwing curves. That made a big difference."

The catcher-pitcher relationship is equally critical in another area: throwing out base-stealers. One of baseball's most familiar debates is whether a runner steals on the catcher or pitcher. He steals on both. Or neither. Boone was traded from Philadelphia to California in 1982 because he supposedly couldn't throw out runners any more. Suddenly, his arm became a cannon. Actually, the difference wasn't Boone but his pitchers. The Phillie staff had slow moves to the plate. When California won the AL West in 1982, the pitchers threw the ball home in 1.35 seconds on the average, and Boone pegged it to second in 1.9. Few runners can take second in 3.25. As a result, Boone was the only catcher in baseball to throw out more than 50 percent of all would-be base-stealers. He nabbed 58 percent of them. The quickest-armed catcher is Carter, whose throw to second has been timed in 1.8. He could be faster still. "The longer you're in the game, the more you realize how much time you have," he says. "You don't have to rush the throw. I remember making stupid errors on base-stealers I had no chance to get. I threw anyway. If there's no chance to get a guy, there's no reason to throw. When I do throw, I try to throw from wherever I am, even in a crouched position. If you straighten up, you tend to throw high. Just take it back by your ear and go right through."

Catchers also help their pitchers by making strikes of pitches that actually may have been outside the strike zone. Boone holds his glove on the outside corner of the plate and catches the ball in the webbing with men on base or allows it to bounce off with the bases empty. Others guide the pitch back into the strike zone as gently as if they were catching an egg. "This is the best bunch of catchers I've ever worked with," says American League umpire Dale Ford, who has been in the league since 1975. "Guys like Fisk, Martinez, Boone, and Sundberg. Instead of going out and getting the ball, they just ease it back over the plate. You have to be very alert to see it's a ball." These catchers are equally slick with their words. When they disagree with an umpire, they rarely turn around and confront him. That would just get his back up. Instead, they'll make their points while calling signals or returning from a conference on the mound.

With all these skills to perfect, the last thing a catcher needs to do is take his batting woes onto the field. That was the rap on Carter for the first 11 years of his career. "It was so obvious," says a former teammate of his in Montreal. "If he was having a 4-for-4 day, he'd be all gung-ho behind the plate. If he wasn't hitting, he'd just slap down the signs without thinking." Carter came of age in 1985, his first season with the Mets. Playing in constant pain—one bad knee, one bruised thumb, two broken ribs—he lost 12 pounds to take pressure off his knees, caught 143 games, and never asked to be taken out of the lineup. Whether or not he was hitting, he also concentrated on his catching, keeping notebooks on every hitter his staff faced,[2] creatively calling pitches, handling pitchers intelligently. Like most veteran catchers, Carter changed his signals several times a game. The previous season the Cubs had stolen signs from

2. Old-time catchers relied on recall. "I can't remember your name," Bill Dickey told one Joe Gantenbein, a hitter he'd faced several years earlier. "But I know we used to pitch you high and outside."

young Mike Fitzgerald of the Mets and scored 32 runs in a critical four-game series. In 1985 the Mets stayed in the race until the final weekend.

Twelve of the 13 times catchers have been named Most Valuable Player by the Baseball Writers' Association of America they've had eye-popping offensive years. A catcher's defense is rarely noticed, unless he throws out a runner or is involved in a bone-jarring collision at home. His fielding statistics aren't particularly arresting; indeed, the most revealing are probably the ERA of the pitchers he works with and the batting averages of the hitters he works against. The catcher makes himself useful in more subtle ways: a little shake of the glove to position a fielder just where the batter will hit the ball; the right words of encouragement when a pitcher needs them; a perfect call on a key pitch (one of the great calls of all time was a fastball down the middle that Yogi Berra ordered for Ted Williams; the Splendid Splinter was so shocked by this easy-to-hit pitch that he popped it up). More than any player on the team, the catcher is the master technician. It's his responsibility to figure out when the other team will hit-and-run, so that he can call a pitchout; to know how to work pitchers and hitters, and how to convince a reluctant manager to remove a shaky hurler. "The infield is like a steel net held in the hand of a catcher," Jacques Barzun wrote. "He is the psychologist and historian for the staff—or else his signals will give the opposition hits."

"A lot of times a catcher will help a pitcher who has crossed him up and thrown a pitch he didn't call," says Ray Miller, the Minnesota manager and former Baltimore pitching coach. "They'll go off the field, the manager will be mad as hell, and the catcher will say, 'I screwed up.'"

"A catcher can help a pitcher through a tough pitch or a tough inning," says Kansas City manager Dick Howser, "but when you think about it, that can be a major contribution."

A case in point was the Royal-Yankee game of April 9, 1986. KC catcher Sundberg dealt with every type of pitcher: one who wasn't sharp, one who was, and reliever Dan ("That's Entertainment") Quisenberry, whose every outing is an adventure. In the first inning the score was 1-1 and KC's lefthanded starter Charlie Leibrandt had runners on second and third with one out. Facing the prospect of pitching to righthanded batters Gary Roenicke, Henry Cotto, and Dale Berra, Leibrandt was in danger of letting the game get out of hand.

"What you want to do in this situation is keep the batter off the plate so that he can't hit the ball to the outfield," said Sundberg. "Roenicke likes the fastball out over the plate, where he can extend his arms; we threw fastballs in and changeups away." Unfortunately, Leibrandt's control was off, and Roenicke walked to load the bases. Using much the same thinking against Cotto and Berra, Leibrandt induced Cotto to ground into a force play (with a run scoring), Dale Berra to foul out. The Yankees had taken a 2-1 lead, but none of the three righthanders had hit the ball out of the infield. The game was still in hand.

The Royals went ahead 5-2, and New York fought back, scored twice, and kayoed Leibrandt in the fourth. In came reliever Steve Farr with a runner on third and the ever-dangerous Dave Winfield at bat. "I let Jim call all the pitches," said Farr. A good thing. On 2-1, Sundberg called an inside fastball, and Winfield, who steps into every pitch, was nearly hit and was sent sprawling. On 3-1, Sundberg switched to a curve on the outside corner. A classic catcher's gambit: using one pitch to set up another. Having expected a pitch over the plate, Winfield lunged at the ball, hit it off the end of his bat, and grounded weakly to the pitcher. The runner on third never scored.

Farr pitched one-hit ball for 4⅔ innings and left in the ninth with a 7-4 lead. Whereupon Quisenberry put runners on the corners with two outs and Winfield again batting. "All we try to do in a situation like this is stay down and away and keep the ball in the park," said Sundberg. Quisenberry threw six sinkers and struck out Winfield on a 3-2 pitch to end the game.

Sundberg took little credit. "We were doing very basic stuff," he said. He smiled ruefully and thought about the previous day's game in which the Yankees' Butch Wynegar had beaten the Royals with a three-run homer. "Here's where the catcher can make a difference. With two outs and a 3-2 count, we were looking for dead red—something hard to throw him. The thinking was: he's not a home run threat since he hit only eight last year, and if we finesse him and miss, the bases are loaded. At least, that was how our pitcher, Bud Black, felt. I felt a fastball was the one pitch Wynegar could drive. I had called for a changeup, but Bud wanted a fastball. I went along with him, and Wynegar hit it out.

"I tossed and turned about that pitch. If there's one thing I've learned from experience, it's to go with strong instincts. I should have gone out to the mound and said, 'I really don't think you should call that pitch.'"

Boone knows exactly what Sundberg means about instinct.

"I view pitching and catching as less of a science than an art form," Boone says. "You might have a pitcher who's having trouble with a breaking ball, so you'll throw them early when he won't get hurt by one that hangs. You work up to a point where you can use them in pressure situations. The most important thing is to stay with the pitcher's strength, not the batter's weakness. But I can't explain what I do. Things happen. All of a sudden you're going with pitches you never thought you'd call for."

In all, the catcher has a unique position on the field. He's the only man squatting instead of standing, positioning himself in foul territory instead of fair, viewing all eight teammates at once, wearing heavy equipment. He must be durable, patient, stoic, tough, thoughtful, thorough, self-possessed, strong, flexible, loyal, reverent, true, and brave. He's the captain, the quarterback, the signal-caller, the natural for a future manager's job (e.g., Yogi Berra, Connie Mack, Al Lopez, Paul Richards). And that's only fair. "By the time you've learned it all," former catcher Dave Duncan told the *New Yorker*'s Roger Angell, "by the time you're really proficient, you're almost too old to go on catching."

For such a taxing position, catching has exceptionally genteel roots. Early catchers didn't squat and take pitches on the fly; they'd stand 50 feet behind the plate and retrieve balls on a bounce. In the 1860s a player named Nat Hicks became the first catcher to stand directly behind the batter. Others reluctantly followed his example. Working barehanded, barechested, and barefaced except for molded rubber noseguards and teethguards, they built up a most ungentlemanly collection of concussions, lacerated palms, and split lips. In 1875 a Harvard player named Fred W. Thayer invented the mask—actually he adapted a fencer's mask to baseball. In the mid-1880s catchers began using heavy, round gloves—there's debate whether Joe Gunson or Harry Decker was the mitt's inventor. Chest protectors followed, and Roger Bresnahan is usually given credit for using the first shinguards, in 1907. A 1920s catcher, Muddy Ruel, coined the term "tools of ignorance" to describe his 20 pounds of equipment. They were, of course, the tools of intelligence.

Strategy kept pace with equipment. In the 1880s catchers began signaling pitches and realigning infielders. Buck Ewing, who caught from 1880 to 1897, was probably the first to work from a crouch. Ray Schalk (1912–29) popularized backing up first on grounders. Nonetheless, catching was a relatively primitive art until recent times. There was no flashing of one, two, three, or four fingers—just the ace (fastball) and deuce (curve). Most pitchers couldn't get a breaking ball over when behind on the count. Today pitch selection is more complicated, because both hitters and pitchers are more talented. Catchers must constantly gird themselves for throws to second or third, because runners are strikingly faster, too. A typical catcher's quandary: "If I order a fastball on 3-1, the hitter will be waiting; if I don't, the runner will be stealing."

By and large, the modern catcher isn't as hardheaded with pitchers as his predecessor was. "Give him a kick in the pants!" managers used to scream. On one memorable occasion, that's exactly what Hall of Famer Mickey Cochrane did to Rube Walberg. Now listen to Johnny Bench describe *his* system. "There were different personalities. There was the guy you patted on the back, the guy you had to tell about different situations, and the guy you just told, 'Let's go.'"

Modern catchers aren't quite so hard on themselves either. True, LA's Mike Scioscia is considered baseball's best at blocking the plate, because he never gives ground. "He doesn't get out of there like a lot of catchers," says manager Tommy Lasorda. But the comfortable, hinged-pocket glove and the one-handed "Olé!" tag pioneered by Bench have people thinking. Says Sundberg, who was knocked out when he stood too long in front of an American Legion runner, "Catchers used to do it like a linebacker: 'Look at how macho I am.' That's ridiculous. You just got hurt, missed a few weeks, and set back the team. The idea in blocking the plate is to get in and out as quickly as you can. There's no reason why you can't make the play like a shortstop or second baseman. What you do is put your foot on a corner of the plate and give the runner the rest of it. That way he won't crash into you. He'll slide, and he'll probably hookslide. Since the shortest distance between two points is a straight line, you've got him taking the long way."

And giving the catcher one of his few painless moments.

JOHNNY BENCH

Johnny Bench changed catching more than any player influenced any position in baseball history. He revolutionized the way catchers caught, modernized the equipment they used, altered the very way they were perceived.

Johnny Bench applies the tag in no uncertain fashion in the 1974 World Series against the Oakland A's. *National Baseball Library*

Before Bench, catchers were treated in a manner ranging from condescension to contempt. They were viewed as dull-witted, sad-eyed sluggards; the paradigm was Yogi Berra, who was always known for his malapropisms, rarely for his highly intelligent baseball mind. Catchers were certainly slow in one regard: getting to the Hall of Fame. Few made it during their lifetimes—witness Roger Bresnahan (48 years after retirement), Ray Schalk (43), Ernie Lombardi (40), Gabby Hartnett (33), Bill Dickey (22), Josh Gibson (26).

Bench made catching into a glamorous profession. Talk about respect. His most telling statistic may be the fact that he only once led National League catchers in assists. The reason is simple: runners were so scared of Bench that they hesitated to steal. In the first game of the 1976 World Series, New York's Mickey Rivers tried to take second. Bench threw him out, and New York manager Billy Martin didn't order another steal until the Series was lost. The Reds won in four, and Bench was Most Valuable Player. Fast enough to hit inside-the-park homers, he demonstrated that catchers could hit and run as well as field and throw. "I liked being able to win a game four different ways," he says. "Call a good game, throw out runners, get base hits, and block home plate." What Bench didn't mention was his extraordinary agility. Topped balls and bunts that normally went for hits became grist for Bench's nimble feet and lightning arm.

Bench popularized the use of the light, oval-shaped hinged mitt with the crease across the palm—a radical change from the heavy, round gloves with small pockets in the middle. The new gloves presented a larger catching pocket. Taking his cue from the Cubs' Randy Hundley, Bench also popularized the one-handed catch. Others caught the ball in their left hand and immediately slapped the nearby right hand over it. The style subjected the right hand to injury and necessitated a bulky three-step throwing procedure—catch the ball, grab it, cock the throwing arm. With the new style, Bench grabbed the ball and whipped it to his cocked right hand in virtually one motion. His hands were so large he could hold seven baseballs in them; he always, almost automatically, gripped the ball across the seams.

Bench's father, Ted, a former minor league catcher, taught him to throw double the 127 feet from home to second, and throw to specific targets like belt buckles. No wonder Bench could fire to second from a crouch. He threw like a pitcher and wasn't afraid of pitchers, possibly because he had been a 16-1 pitcher himself in high school. Once Bench reached out his bare hand, caught a weak fastball thrown by Jerry Arrigo, and fired it back at greater speed. Arrigo got the message and improved his delivery. Bench knew just how far to push his pitchers. "He'll come out to the mound and treat me like a two-year-old," Cincinnati pitcher Jim Maloney told sportswriter William Barry Furlong, "but so help me, I like it."

Motivated by extraordinary confidence and a healthy fear of failure, Bench had a pressure-resistant personality. He predicted that he'd be Rookie of the Year and the first $100,000 catcher; he was right on both counts. He doesn't have to predict immediate selection to the Hall of Fame; that's guaranteed.

Bench set catchers' records by winning 10 Gold Gloves and hitting 389 home runs, and he worked 1,744 games behind the plate to finish fourth after Al Lopez (1,913), Rick Farrell (1,865), and Gabby Hartnett (1,790) among retired players. Bench could have placed higher in the latter category, but he chose to limit his catching starts to two a week in 1981 when his body told him to slow down. Two years later, departing from the more usual practice, Bench walked away from the game while he could still walk in good health. If his example encourages future catchers to quit before suffering disabling injuries, Johnny's retirement may have been his greatest contribution of all.

5

First Base: Sanctuary or State of Siege?

Nothing gives rise to such wild surmise as the aged ballplayer with first in his eyes. They come flocking to first: from third, from the outfield, from catcher, from weak legs, from ineffectiveness at other positions. They anticipate respite. Then surmise gives way to surprise.

In 1985 Philadelphia third baseman Mike Schmidt moved to first for a season and barely survived his debut there. On his first play he was forced to execute an extreme stretch-and-split. "I've never had to stretch like that since I've been in baseball," he said afterward, icing his left knee. "I felt something weird in the knee, and this ice is just to make sure I can go out there tomorrow night." Schmidt played errorless ball in his first six games but found that the concentration sapped his hitting. He went 4-for-22.

"I enjoyed first because you were in the play more," says Hall of Famer Harmon Killebrew, who also switched there from third midway through his career. "It was dangerous, though. I dislocated my elbow when I collided with a runner while reaching for a bad throw. I should have let the ball go. And I suffered a ruptured hamstring in the 1968 All-Star Game when the soil around first in the Astrodome gave out under my feet."

First can be dangerous for anyone playing it. A righthander reaching down the line with his glove hand is ripe for getting smacked by a baserunner. The same thing has happened to left-handed first basemen reaching across their bodies, even the graceful Keith Hernandez (see profile at end of chapter). And there's no escape for the first baseman who has to reach behind the runner for a poor pickoff throw; he risks getting socked by the runner if he goes for the throw, or missing the ball if he doesn't.

Pain is only one of the surprises in store for refugees from other positions. They expected to rest their weary bones and heavy legs at the new position. Instead they discover its pitfalls. They should have known better. The first baseman accepts an unrivaled number of chances (up to 2,000 a year) and handles the ball more than anyone but the catcher and pitcher.

On most plays he's taking hurried putout throws from infielders while keeping his foot on the bag. When a throw goes astray, the first baseman is faced with difficult plays and decisions. In-the-dirt throw: "Do I sweep at it on the short hop or give with it and risk an in-between hop?" High throw: "Do I try to keep a toe on the bag and stretch for it, or do I leap for it and hope I land on the bag?" Wide or high throw to the home plate side: "Do I stretch for it, or do I leave the bag and tag the runner?"

The most common plight is what to do with a throw in the dirt. "Better to sweep at it than give with it," says former White Sox hitting coach Mike Lum, a onetime big-league first baseman. "You always want the short hop over the in-between one." The team whose first basemen seem to have best mastered the play over the years is the Dodgers. Witness Gil Hodges, Wes Parker, Steve Garvey (another switchee from third). But topnotch personnel is only half the reason. The team's hard-working infield coaches have long used a mechanical arm similar to a pitching machine to make bad throws to first basemen and other infielders in spring training. Hundreds of bad throws. Thousands of them.

"Scoops are satisfying," says Hernandez. "Sometimes it's enough just to block the ball with your body and keep it in the infield. If you do that with a runner on second, he won't score. You keep the ball in front of you, like a catcher with a pitch in the dirt. If you stick a guy at first at the end of his career, a lot of balls in the dirt get by and runners reach base; if they're already on, they might score. You can lose a lot of games that way."

First takes years to learn. Awaiting a throw from pitcher Tom Seaver on a sacrifice play, the White Sox' young Greg Walker saw the ball and runner converging five or six feet to his left. Let him describe what happened next. "I should have caught the ball and given the runner the base. Instead, I tried to catch the ball and tag the runner." He missed both and the deciding run scored from second.

The necessary skills mount up. The term "pick it" often refers to a first baseman, who must pick those throws out of the dirt and pick those hard smashes too. A good first baseman can bluff a runner back to the bag or cut behind him for a pickoff throw. The Orioles' Eddie Murray excels at both. Then there are the throws a first baseman himself must make: throws to second, occasional throws to third or the plate, many, many throws to his pitcher on the 3-1 play. Suddenly, the initiate begins to perceive first as a skill position. Unquestionably it's a position for people who like to be in the thick of things. That's why it's Pete Rose's favorite.

"First base is a tremendous position," he says. "You're more involved there than anywhere but catcher. Every time an infielder throws a ball, you probably have a chance to touch it. We had a game in Philadelphia where I had 16 putouts without a ground ball hit to me. That's why I disagree with people who want to put a guy who can't catch there. What's the sense of having Gold Glove infielders when the guy at first is going to miss their throws? You can't hide from the baseball; the ball will find you."

"A good first baseman like Cecil Cooper or Don Mattingly can save a game as well as a shortstop can," says the quintessential American League utilityman Greg Pryor. "There are so many tough plays—picking the ball out of the dirt, going to your right and then throwing to the pitcher, throwing to second when a guy has been picked off first. You have to anticipate that situation and move into the infield so that you can throw to second without hitting the runner. Eddie Murray does that as well as anyone."

"When you throw the ball to second, you want to get rid of it as fast as possible," says Hernandez, who usually leads National League first basemen in double plays. "You throw it over the top and short-arm it. But the main thing is to throw it straight. You don't want to throw a sinker to the shortstop."

"You have to think on every play," says former National League first baseman Bill White. "You need quick feet to chase down pop-ups and run down sacrifice bunts. Making the pickup depends more than anything on keeping your eye on the ball. The toughest play is chasing a bunt and making the throw to second, especially when a lefthanded pull hitter is up. They can fake the bunt and knock your teeth out. Once even a right-handed pitcher crossed me up and swung away. The ball went shooting by my head, and I laughed like hell."

Most of the time first basemen don't find bunts or the 3-6-3 double play routine. On the DP, a righthanded first baseman must field the ball and pivot before throwing, while a left-hander can field and throw in the same motion. Granted, the reverse is true on the 3-1 play, but that involves a much shorter throw. There have been many smooth-fielding righthanders, such as Garvey, Hodges, George Scott, Vic Power, and Murray, to go with such legendary lefthanders as Hernandez, George Sisler, Mickey Vernon, Parker, and Ferris Fain. Nonetheless, first is the only position that absolutely, positively favors the lefty.

Not that the 3-6-3 double play is easy for anyone. To field a ball, throw one way, then grope backward for the base and a return throw requires a special kind of rhythm. "Waltz, waltz, waltz," the lefthanded Lou Gehrig used to say to himself as he struggled to master the play. He never fully succeeded. "Me no waltz," the Puerto Rican-born Power told *Sports Illustrated*'s Herm Weiskopf years later. "I cha-cha-cha." Even so, there's probably nothing quite so awkward as the 3-6-3 play at first.

That's not all that makes first unique. A first baseman may suffer the ultimate fielding embarrassment. Imagine missing a simple throw! It didn't wash when the Yankees' Joe Pepitone protested that white shirts in the stands distracted him in the 1963 World Series. He missed a throw right at him, and the error helped cost the Yankees the final run of the final game.

Dick Stuart, by contrast, reveled in his own incompetence. Variously known as "Dr. Strangeglove," "Stonefingers," and "Clank," for the sound of the ball coming off his glove, he led or tied all major league first basemen in errors every season from 1958 to 1961. Stuart didn't mind. "Errors are part of my image," he'd brag. "One night in Pittsburgh, thirty thousand fans gave me a standing ovation when I caught a hot dog wrapper on the fly."

First is more fun if the practitioner is as loquacious as Stuart. While strong, silent types like Murray and Steve Balboni do fine at first, it's a uniquely convivial position, what with all those baserunners to exchange the time of day with. A kibitzer's position, really, although some first basemen will try to distract the runner and set him up for a pickoff. "Look up at that blimp!" Pirate first baseman Willie Stargell said to Baltimore baserunner Doug DeCinces during the 1979 Series. "Willie," said DeCinces, "it's the World Series!" That's not the only psychological stratagem first basemen use on runners. Sometimes they'll take several pickoff throws from the pitcher and return them without bothering to tag. Then they'll fake-throw and tag the runner as he leaves the base. Detroit's Dave Bergman fooled Baltimore's Alan Wiggins that way.

There's no glove quite as lovely as the oval now in use at first. And there's no sight in baseball quite as graceful as that of a first baseman stretching forward, one foot on the nearest corner of the bag, glove hand extended as he takes a high throw on a close play: vintage *Winged Victory*. The stretch is what artistically ennobles the position. Hence, Hall of Famer Willie (Stretch) McCovey, one of the best ever.

In their greatest moments, however, first basemen don't always look graceful. They're often sprawled on the ground after diving to field a line drive or hard grounder. Mets' fans swear they see Keith Hernandez make a play or two like that every game, but such moments of greatness aren't reserved for the best first basemen alone. In the 1984 playoffs Detroit's Darrell Evans, yet another converted third baseman, made just such a stop on KC's Willie Wilson. It pretty well wrapped up the third and final game.

"When he switched from left late in his career, Carl Yastrzemski made a diving play on me that reminded me of Brooks Robinson at third," says Ken Harrelson. "He went four or five feet into foul territory to pick up a hard grounder, scrambled to his feet, and threw a strike to the shortstop for the force at second. The pitcher thought the ball had gone through for a hit and hadn't come over, so Carl scrambled back and arrived at first at the same time as the ball to double me up."

There was a more famous sprawling play in a September 15, 1940, doubleheader between the Yankees and St. Louis Browns. The Browns had won the opener 10-5 and were leading in the second game 2-0, with New York's Buddy Rosar on first and no outs in the seventh. When Babe Dahlgren squared around to bunt, St. Louis first baseman George McQuinn charged in. Dahlgren immediately crossed him up and hit a sharp liner to the right side. The lefthanded McQuinn dove, short-hopped the ball, and threw from a prone position to force Rosar at second. That would have sufficed, but McQuinn leaped up and raced Dahlgren to first. Though the throw by shortstop Johnny Berardino[1] was low and down the first-base line, McQuinn grabbed the ball behind his body, slid, and tagged first ahead of the run-

---

1. Who later became a semifamous actor.

Star first basemen of the pre-modern era: Roger Connor, top, and Jake Beckley. *National Baseball Library*

An excellent case can be made for all three of these players as among the finest-fielding first basemen of all time: Hal Chase, top left; Fred Tenney, top right; and George Sisler, bottom left. *National Baseball Library*

ner. It's said that the sight of McQuinn looking up from the ground to get the "out" call haunted the Yankees for the rest of the season, and they finished two games out after winning four consecutive pennants. Maybe that's why they acquired Mc-Quinn later in his career.

In baseball's early days first basemen weren't so agile. They were expected to stand on first and wait. Literally. They weren't asked to field the ball or throw it, just catch it. Charles (The Old Roman) Comiskey wasn't, as stated on his Hall of Fame plaque, the first to play off the bag, but he was among the best of his time. Old Reliable Joe Start, who probably *was* the first off the bag, nonetheless had only 13 assists among 732 chances in 1878. Failed third baseman Cap Anson may have introduced the stretch, as claimed, but he also perfected the bobble. "Big Roger" Connor, all 6'3", 220 pounds of him, was remarkably agile. Connor was an anomaly; most first basemen of the time were small and stationary.

The best turn-of-the century first baseman, Fred Tenney of the Boston Beaneaters, probably popularized the one-handed catch and began making the 3-6-3 double play. Equally nimble was Chick Gandil, who got entirely too nimble when he engineered the Black Sox scandal. Frank Chance, as in Tinkers-to-Ever-to, fully merited his poetic status. But the real pioneer among modern first basemen was Prince Hal Chase (1905–19). He was so quick he could make 3-5 throws to third on attempted sacrifices, and he occasionally fielded squeeze bunts and tagged both the batter and runner coming home.

There followed a slew of Hall of Famers—George Sisler, Lou Gehrig, Bill Terry, Hank Greenberg, Jimmie Foxx, Buck Leonard, and others. Some, like Terry and all-time assist leader Sisler,[2] were naturals. Others like Greenberg and Gehrig laboriously learned the position. But there were still too many incredible bulks out there, situated at first exclusively to keep their bats in the lineup. Sisler was infuriated by that practice; he argued that too many chances come a first baseman's way for the position to be a liability. Sisler might have pointed proudly to Edward Joseph (Big Ed) Konetchy, who handled 19 chances for the Dodgers in their celebrated 26-inning game with the Braves, and 19 in another game for a World Series record, both in 1920. But Konetchy wasn't the norm.

Indeed, it's impossible to trace a steady improvement in the play of first basemen. As late as the 1960s we had embarrassments like Steve Bilko.[3] Today's first basemen are far better fielders, but from the beginning the best have invariably been switchees: Cecil Cooper and Don Mattingly from the outfield, Sisler from pitcher, Chase from various infield positions. Moreover, good first basemen are often switched elsewhere. Competent fielders who were trained to play first and remained there —Kent Hrbek and Keith Hernandez, to name two—are still the exception.

First is challenging enough to deserve homegrown players. Switched there for a game to rest his weary centerfielder's legs,

2. Sisler had 1,528 assists and may have deserved another. On one play he fielded the ball and lobbed to the pitcher covering first. When he realized there was no pitcher covering first, Sisler caught his own throw and stepped on the bag.

3. Not to mention Marvelous Marv Throneberry of the early Mets. "We was going to get you a birthday cake," manager Casey Stengel told him, "but we figured you'd drop it."

Joe DiMaggio struggled painfully. Afterward someone asked sympathetically if it had been his first game at first. Not only was it his first, DiMaggio replied, it was also his last.

KEITH HERNANDEZ

Like Brooks Robinson at third, first baseman Keith Hernandez has set a standard for his position and dramatically affected every infield he's played for. Robinson's range at third enabled his shortstop to shade toward second, his second baseman to move closer to first, and his first baseman to guard the line. Hernandez has the same effect, except in reverse. When there's no runner on first, he plays perhaps a third of the way toward second. One reason the Mets' defense was so successful in 1986 was that Hernandez gave second baseman Wally Backman the freedom to move closer to second and steal would-be singles up the middle.

Hernandez is no speed merchant, but it's doubtful any first baseman ever had his range. It's almost inconceivable that anyone has studied the position more closely. Ask him why he plays so far off the bag and he'll cite the relative scarcity of left-handed pull hitters in the National League and the fact that righthanders rarely hit down the right-field line. Watch him awaiting a pitch, with his open glove close to the ground. Most first basemen's mitts are pointing slightly to the side; Hernandez holds his facing the middle of the plate, like a hockey goalie in search of a puck. Observe him guarding a runner. His left foot is nearly in foul territory, allowing him to get his right (glove) hand down directly in front of the base to make the tag on a pickoff play. Precise, analytical.

Although many a player hides a weak throwing arm at first, Hernandez showcases his own strong arm. No one throws better to other bases. On extra-base hits down the right-field line, he has at times been the relay man, an honor normally reserved for second basemen. No first baseman makes a better throw from the hole to the pitcher covering first. "I look at the play as a quick-in to a wide receiver," says Hernandez, a former high school quarterback. "You have to lead him and put something on it." A play Hernandez remembers fondly was a 1984 high hopper Pittsburgh's Lee Lacy hit in the hole that Hernandez jumped for while moving toward second. He caught the ball in the air, spun, and threw a strike to pitcher Walt Terrell.

No Hernandez history would be complete without mention

Exhibition action: the Mets' Keith Hernandez has just taken a throw in an attempt to tag the Yankees' Bobby Meacham.
Matthew L. Kaplan

of the times he's cut to the opposite side of the pitcher's mound to grab a bunt and fire to third, or caught high hoppers bare-handed and made throws home. Incredibly, he's even studied the best ways to make the rare barehanded play. "It's not so much getting the ball in your hand as throwing it in the same motion," he says. "You have to adjust the throw to the grip because you won't always have the ball in your fingers when you catch it." In 1985 Hernandez had 139 assists; the next closest National League first baseman had 107.

Hernandez has been playing first base steadily since his Little League days. His father, John, a retired firefighter and former minor league first baseman, decided that the lefthanded Keith should play first when he wasn't pitching. "He'd take me to Candlestick Park every time Bill White came into town with the Phillies or Cardinals, and we'd study his footwork, fielding, and throwing," Hernandez says.

Hernandez kept studying the position—through school, through the minors, and through his major league career with the Cardinals and Mets. "He is," veteran Rusty Staub told the *New York Times*'s Craig Wolff, "the most intense player I've ever played with."

6

Second Base: Second Place?

The moment every second baseman cherishes: bases loaded, two outs in the seventh inning, and the Yankees holding a 4-2 lead over the Dodgers in the seventh game of the 1952 World Series. Jackie Robinson hits a high pop on a 3-2 pitch, and the ball virtually disappears in the Ebbets Field sun. While the ball is still in the air, first baseman Joe Collins loses sight of it, pitcher Bob Kuzava stands helplessly on the mound, two Dodgers cross the plate and another rounds third. Ah, but at the last instant, Billy Martin, the feistiest of all second basemen, runs toward the mound, reaches desperately for the ball, and spears it knee-high. Robinson is out, the Yankees go on to win 4-2, and the Series is saved. By a second baseman.

"That happens a lot," second basemen will tell you, "and we don't get much credit." They have a point. Only third base, with eight players in the Hall of Fame, has fewer immortals than the nine second basemen. There should be more.

Unfortunately, one can easily overlook second base. It's the only position best suited for a player under six feet, dexterity being more important than size or strength when you're executing that mambo in the pivot. Little guys are always going to be shunted to second and forgotten. Additionally, second is considered the secondary partner in the double play combination. Kansas City's Frank White, one of the best recent second basemen, disputes that. Second base, claims White, is a tougher position than short!

Before we respond emotionally and indignantly, let's hear him out. "It's true that the shortstop has a longer throw," says White, "but the second baseman has to make the pivot more often. And he has a much tougher pivot. He's a stationary target, and he doesn't actually see the runner until he's made the throw to first. The shortstop has the play in front of him. That's why a second baseman has to be a better athlete.

"If the ball's slowly hit to the shortstop or third baseman and he throws to second, the second baseman has to decide whether to make the double play or make the force and get out of the way. A second baseman has to have a lot of belief. He has to believe he's going to get hit, and he has to believe it's not going to hurt. Actually, I've only been hit hard twice while making the pivot. That's because I don't keep going across the base. I straddle it when I'm taking the throw, and I use it for protection when I'm making my own throw. So I'm either behind the bag or over it."

White's preoccupation with the pivot is understandable. The scene of the second baseman vaulting over the sliding runner is probably the most evocative in baseball. It's the most photographed, or at least the most photographable; check the covers of *Sports Illustrated* during the World Series. It's also the most heartrending. Taking one throw and making another on the same play leaves the second baseman the most vulnerable player in the game: the guy whose knee could be turned into jelly by a blind-side block. Incredibly, second basemen treat the threat of serious injury like so much dandruff to flick off their collars. "You don't think about it," they say. But *we* should think about the second baseman who has best avoided injury in those touchy situations. The Louie Lightfoot Award, based on observation, eyewitness testimony, hearsay, and personal prejudice, goes to Julian (The Phantom) Javier of the 1960–72 Cardinals and Reds. "Outstanding," says one of his shortstops, Dal Maxvill. "Like a ghost. Dancing in the air."

Happily, the pivot play is not quite as treacherous as it used to be. After KC's Hal McRae executed a roll-block slide into the Yankee's Willie Randolph in the 1977 playoffs, officials wrote into their rulebook what has become known as the McRae Rule: "A sliding runner must hit ground before the bag." What's more, interference is now called when "any batter or runner who has just been put out hinders or impedes any following play being made on a runner. Such runner shall be declared out for the interference of his teammate." (In practice, the runner is usually allowed to slide three feet on either side of second.) In return for this restriction, however, fielders are now expected to stop executing, and umpires to stop tolerating, the "phantom tag." In the days when runners had open season on pivotmen, the runners were called out any time the ball reached the fielder before they did. Fielders were allowed to make their relays before stepping on second, or step off before catching the ball. No more. So they still run the risk of getting hit. One of the critical decisions a second baseman must make is when to make the relay and when to settle for the force and "eat the ball." Many are the second basemen who have insisted on throwing while getting hit, and have launched the ball into the stands.

The pivot play is only the most visible of a second baseman's responsibilities. He can be as busy handling signals and repositioning fielders as the shortstop—more so in White's case because he has usually been more experienced than the guy to his right. It's often assumed that the shortstop gets more chances than the second baseman. That's only true on ground balls. Because the second baseman must make both a putout and an assist on most double plays, and because he handles so many throws at second on steals and at first base on sacrifices, he takes an average of about five chances a game to four for the shortstop.

The second baseman also seems to catch more pop-ups in foul ground than the shortstop, probably because he's covering for the first baseman, instead of the more mobile third baseman. In a 1985 game at Texas, Boston second baseman Marty Barrett had just ended the top half of an inning as a baserunner involved in a jarring collision at home when he began the bottom half by chasing a foul pop, catching it, and tumbling over the fence. Houston manager Hal Lanier, who played all the infield positions, recalls a time as a Giant second baseman when he ran over a sand bullpen mound, made an excellent catch, bounced off a fence, and threw out a runner who had tagged at first.

Unquestionably, the shortstop has a longer, tougher throw to first on grounders. The second baseman invariably has a short throw and the luxury to recover after bobbling a ball and still get his mark. Nonetheless, he doesn't have such an easy time of it. He's forever changing directions, crablike. At times you'll see him skittering to his left to take balls in the hole, turn all the way round and throw to second for the 4-6 force or to first for the 4-3 putout; no one has done that better than Frank White. Or he'll go behind second base to backhand a ball and then somehow throw to first while his momentum is going the other way. "Tommy Herr makes that play as well as anyone," says Lanier, who coached Herr in St. Louis. "He goes to his right and throws off his right foot without taking the time to plant it." Others can't make the play without planting, but that can take the extra split second that makes a fast runner safe.

There's a certain nobility to second base. Perfect games being so rare, the very fulcrum of a contest is preventing the inevitable baserunner from reaching second base: quite literally, "scoring position." The play of the second baseman is at the heart of this struggle. All this, and second basemen consistently hit better than shortstops!

Almost from the beginning, second basemen have been reluctant handmaidens to shortstops. In the early nineteenth century the shortstop was positioning himself all over the lot: in the outfield to take relays, behind the mound, and finally where he stands today. The second baseman was anchored on his bag. He began coming off it in the 1860s, probably following the example of the first validly pro team, the Cincinnati Red Stockings, who were introducing all manner of modern stratagems. Nonetheless, second basemen weren't properly appreciated. Author John Thorn, an expert on nineteenth-century baseball, finds it incredible that Cincinnati great Bid McPhee, who played from 1882 to 1899 and was the best second baseman of his time, isn't in the Hall.[1]

The indignities have mounted in the twentieth century. Eddie Collins, who did make the Hall, was a converted shortstop. Collins and his Cooperstown brethren had to hit .300 to make it, the exception being the legendary fielder Johnny Evers, who batted .270. When a second baseman's defense is considered at all, it's frequently misunderstood. Entirely too many players are praised for flashy play. The best are those who anticipate well and smartly move in front of grounders instead of lunging for them. Flashy second basemen make noticed plays; smart second basemen make notable plays.

Happily, there's a worthy and simple statistic used in analyzing middle infielders.[2] Actually two stats. In the 1983 *Baseball Research Journal*, a publication of the Society for American Baseball Research (SABR), author Jim McMartin wrote a piece called "Two Measures of Fielding Ability." In it he correctly dis-

1. An article by Bob Carroll in *The National Pastime*, a Thorn-edited baseball review, makes a strong case for McPhee. Between 1882 and 1897, McPhee led his league's second basemen in double plays 11 times, fielding average nine times, putouts eight times, and assists six times, and averaged an impressive 6.7 chances per game over his career. What's more, he played barehanded for all but his last three seasons.

2. An equally worthy, more complicated system for evaluating all everyday players is presented by John Thorn and Pete Palmer in *The Hidden Game of Baseball*.

When old-timers choose an all-star team for the pre-World War I era, the second baseman is always either Napoleon Lajoie, left, or Eddie Collins.
National Baseball Library

missed fielding percentage as the be-all and end-all of fielding stats. "Fielding percentage doesn't evaluate range," said McMartin. "The basic problem is that a fielder is not charged with an error when he is simply too slow to get to the ball." McMartin developed two additional measures. The first he called "fielding effectiveness." He calculated it by multiplying two numbers: Bill James's range factor (putouts and assists divided by games played), and a system of measuring double play effectiveness that involves subtracting errors from DPs. The final equation, math majors, is $FE = (PO+A)/G \times (1 + (DP-E/G))$.

McMartin's second statistical index is called a "leader index." He calculated it by adding the number of times a fielder led his league in putouts, assists, and double plays, subtracting the number of times he led in errors, and dividing what's left by the number of seasons times three. A player would receive the maximum 100 percent score if he led every year in putouts, assists, and double plays and never in errors.

McMartin analyzed the records of all middle infielders who played at least 100 games a year for four or more seasons. The results, by decade:

Fielding effectiveness—Napoleon Lajoie, Philadelphia Athletics and Cleveland, 1900s; Eddie Collins, Philadelphia Athletics and Chicago White Sox, 1910s; Hughie Critz, Cincinnati, 1920s; Ski Melillo, St. Louis Browns, 1930s; Bobby Doerr, Boston Red Sox, 1940s; Red Schoendienst, St. Louis Cardinals, New York Giants, and Milwaukee Braves, 1950s; Bill Mazeroski, Pittsburgh, 1960s; Bobby Grich, Baltimore and California, 1970s.

Leader index—Lajoie, 1900s; George Cutshaw, Brooklyn, 1910s; Bucky Harris, Washington, 1920s; Melillo, 1930s; Doerr, 1940s; Nellie Fox, Chicago White Sox, 1950s; Mazeroski, 1960s; Grich, 1970s.

Among the leaders, the only Hall of Famers are Doerr, Lajoie, Collins, and Harris—and Harris made it strictly as a manager. Some of the Hall's omissions are unfortunate enough when you consider that middle infielders are supposed to be defense-oriented, more so when you see the overlooked players' *offensive* stats. Mazeroski had 2,016 lifetime hits and the most dramatic home run in World Series history. Fox had 2,663 hits. Schoendienst had 2,449. And they've been passed over for Cooperstown: Mazeroski and Schoendienst rebuffed year after year, Fox dying without being immortalized. You wonder why second basemen are a little sensitive.

The least we can do is listen to them.

Doerr (1937–51). Had a .288 lifetime average, 223 home runs, and 1,247 runs batted in to go with his 2,042 hits. Led American League second basemen in fielding percentage six times. From June 24 to September 19, 1948, in one of baseball's hottest pennant races, handled 414 consecutive chances without an error. Despite migraine headaches, hit .409 and handled 49 chances flawlessly in 1946 World Series. Coached in Toronto for five seasons and in Toronto farm system for three. Now retired in Oregon mountains. "I wanted more than anything to be Bobby Doerr," says National League President A. Bartlett Giamatti.

"When I came up in 1937, there were no infield coaches and you'd seek information," says Doerr. "I'd talk to Charlie Gehringer of the Tigers a lot. After a while, though, you developed

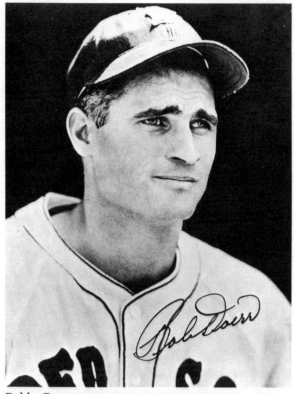

Bobby Doerr. *National Baseball Library*

your own style. Gehringer straddled the bag on the pivot; I'd go across on some plays, step back on others. I never did get hurt. I guess I must have relaxed as they came in. It also helped that they never knew which way I was going.

"At second, you throw everything across your body. That's one of the things that makes it different from short and third. The only time you come over the top is when you're behind second and need to put something extra on it.

"A lot of play at second is instinctive. Sometimes you just know a guy is going to pull a curve or other off-speed pitch, so you take a chance and move to your left when the ball is being thrown.

"There's a lot of talk about second basemen being converted shortstops. What we found is that not every shortstop can come over and make the pivot. A lot of them just can't get used to the runner coming into them from the blind side."

Mazeroski. See profile at the end of this chapter.

Red Schoendienst. *National Baseball Library*

Schoendienst (1945–63). From Germantown, Illinois. Excel-
lent team player, competed in the 1946 Series as a 23-year-old
Cardinal, traded from Giants to Braves in 1957 and immediately
solidified infield to help team win pennant. Led the league seven
times in fielding percentage. At various times also led league in at-
bats, hits, doubles, stolen bases, pinch-hits, and pinch-hit at-bats.
Managed 1967 Cardinals to World Series title, later became team
hitting coach.

"I threw my arm out in Rochester, and it hampered me my
entire career. Fortunately, I got rid of the ball quickly and had a
strong enough arm for second base.

"The most important thing about second is not to look at the
runner and be afraid. It's true you're on the blind side, but it
should make no difference because every runner has to go to

Bobby Grich. *California Angels*

the bag. If you know how a guy runs and slides, you have the advantage. You should also know your shortstop. It's all timing. I always tried to get a step away from the bag and make a stutter-step, because you don't know where the ball will be thrown. I wanted it chest-high. The main thing is to look the ball into your glove before throwing. I guess it's the same in all sports.

"A lot of second basemen go across the bag. Myself and Maz went to it, caught the ball, and threw. I'd move as soon as I threw and go over the top of the runner. I never got hit. Well, almost never. I always thought the toughest play was when the ball was thrown into the dirt and into the runner. You just have to scoop it and settle on the force. Once the third baseman made a throw like that, and Billy Bruton hit me hard. If you're not light on your feet, you'll break a leg. Fortunately, I was agile enough that my weight wasn't on the foot he hit. The best kind of second baseman is as agile as a dancer: a Gene Kelly, a Fred Astaire."

Grich (1970–86). Born in Michigan but has become a Southern Californian through and through. Unusually large for a second baseman at 6'2", 195 pounds. Holds the major league record for most putouts in a season by a second baseman with 484 in 1974. Tied the major league record for fewest errors in a season (800 or more chances) with five in 1973. That year had 945 chances and a .995 fielding percentage. Has been equally sharp as a young player for Orioles and older player for Angels. As a 36-year-old in 1985, made only two errors in 116 games. From 1973 through 1975 led AL second basemen in chances and double plays. In the second-to-last game of the 1974 season, with the Orioles and Yankees fighting for the lead, saved a potential game-losing hit by making a diving, backhanded stab behind second and throwing to shortstop Mark Belanger to start a game-ending double play. Orioles went on to win AL East title. His career fielding percentage (.9839) trailed only Jerry Lumpe's .9844 among second basemen.

"My size can be a disadvantage, because I'm not as quick as smaller men. If I stood tall, it would take too long to get down, so I take a consciously low body position. I concentrate on picking up the ball off the bat. If I just look at the vicinity of the batter, I know I'm not concentrating. Suddenly, the ball's a third of the way to me.

"Size can also work to my advantage. It helps when I have to dive for a ball or go up for a line drive or high throw. Also, runners have second thoughts about hitting me.

"I never catch one-handed unless there's no choice. Two-handed, I can exchange the ball more easily to the bare hand. It's smoother, and I can throw to first in virtually one motion, like a quarterback racing right while throwing left.

"On double plays I always meet the ball with my left foot on the bag. If the right foot were there, my momentum would be toward first too much, and I'd have trouble taking throws to my right."

A couple of hours after he spoke, Grich handled a double play throw well to the right of second. Because his left foot was planted on the bag, he was able to barehand the ball and throw successfully to first without wasting a step. "I thought about what I'd told you when I made that play," he said, smiling, a maestro who had given a perfect demonstration.

We shouldn't overlook Frank White, a Gold Glove winner from 1977 to 1982. In these peak years White was an elegant fielder who inspired poetic tributes. "He's so sweet with his hands and feet," said Yankee second baseman Willie Randolph, a longtime friend and playing foe. "There's nothing herky-jerky, just"—Randolph simulated a quick field-and-throw—"boom-boom. When I see him on the field, I'll say, 'How you doin', idol?'"

Most of the time, fine. Consider the plays White is proudest of:

In the last game of the 1977 playoffs the Royals were nursing a one-run lead, with runners on first and third and two outs, when New York's Chris Chambliss hit a hard grounder up the middle. White made a diving stop and forced Reggie Jackson at second. "Had we gone on to win the game, that play would have been remembered," White says. Instead, the Yankees rallied to win in the ninth.

In the second game of the 1980 playoffs the Royals took a one-run lead into the ninth. Graig Nettles hit a shot that caromed off White's glove. He calmly barehanded the ball in the air and made the throw to first in time.

In the 1980 Series White made an unassisted double play by diving to catch Mike Schmidt's liner and stepping on second ahead of the runner.

White's methodology is unique, to say the least. A graduate of the Royals' now-defunct baseball academy, he learned to take balls off the short hop while aggressively pushing his glove forward; most fielders take the easy hop and cradle the ball. White also learned to field balls with his bare hand on top of the glove instead of behind it. "A lot of bad hops hit you on the chest or on the arm, after hopping over the glove," he says. "What I've been able to do with the grip is force the ball back in the glove with the palm of my right hand.

"I've received every compliment a middle infielder can get, except that I'm smart. They say I have a good arm, speed, range, and the ability to make the double play. But I'm the guy who relays the signs, positions the first baseman, helps the out-fielders and the shortstop. I don't pay much attention to scouting reports because they might be a few days old and the hitter might be trying something new. A lot of scouting reports are based on how a pitcher was doing on a given day. Some managers will make you follow the charts; a good one will give you some freedom. That's why I don't look to the manager and fielding coach, who aren't on the field. I'll speak to the pitcher and catcher to see how the hitter is being pitched. I'll also make some adjustments on my own from studying the hitters. All in all, I play an unorthodox second base."

But what, really, is orthodox? As White and his peers demonstrate, second base can be played in a variety of ways. Their personality types are not as diverse. Some second basemen like Billy Martin are peevish; most of the good ones are stoical. "You could be in a fight every day if you wanted to get even with the runners," says Doerr. "You have to learn to accept getting hit. If you started fighting, they'd be after you every day." The ultimate compliment to a second baseman may have been paid to Charlie Gehringer by Ty Cobb. "He'd say hello at the start of spring training and goodbye at the end of the season, and the rest of the time he'd let his bat and glove do the talking for him."

Maybe second basemen are *too* quiet. Though it was one of only eight unassisted triple plays in baseball history, Bill Wambsganss's epic moment in the 1920 World Series was buried in a spectacular game, a spectacular Series, and Wamby's spectacular modesty. ("The only credit I really take was in making the catch.") Indeed, some remember his feat not for what it accomplished but for the way Ring Lardner described it: "In the next innings Kilduff and Miller got base hits off Bagby 'Master Mind' and Mitchell cleared the bases with a line drive to WWaammbbsshhggannnsh. An expert cuckoo setting in the press box told me it was the 1st time in world series history that a man named Wambsganss had ever made a triple play assisted by consonants only."

Second basemen have the capacity to perform their derring-do, and then vanish in utter silence. Jackie Robinson is remembered for many things, but rarely for the diving, backhanded twelfth-inning catch (and fourteenth-inning homer) that enabled the Dodgers to finish the 1951 season tied with the Giants and force the memorable playoff. The A's Dick Green made spectacular plays in the last three games of the 1974 Series, but didn't receive the official Most Valuable Player award because he went hitless over all five games. Remember Brian Doyle, a hero in the 1978 Series? He subbed for the injured Willie Randolph, starred on offense and defense, and played only 20 games when Randolph returned the next season.

Oh, the quiet dignity of Willie Randolph, the one constant in the Steinbrenner clubhouse! And how about an earlier Yankee, Bobby Richardson, whose greatest contribution was almost totally unappreciated? It was the ninth inning of the 1962 World Series finale: Yanks leading San Francisco, 1-0, Giants on second and third, two outs and Willie McCovey at bat. McCovey hit one of the hardest line drives in the history of postseason play, and Richardson caught it to end the Series. Attention immediately focused on players other than Richardson: on McCovey, on Yankee manager Ralph Houk's decision to pitch to McCovey with first base open, and on rightfielder Roger Maris, whose play holding the previous batter, Willie Mays, to a double had prevented a run from scoring. When the subject of Richardson was broached, people shrugged and said, "The ball was hit right at him."

Not so simple. As McCovey came to bat, Richardson had looked to Houk for directions on where to play the hitter. When managers don't know what to do, they look at their feet. That's what Houk did, and Richardson had to position himself. If he had stood another three feet to his left or right, McCovey might have won the Series with a two-run single.

Richardson's perfect positioning was little noted nor long remembered. He was a second baseman.

BILL MAZEROSKI

Bill Mazeroski had an economical way of handling grounders and questions, so let's not tarry. Hard-scrabble kid from Ohio mining town not far from where Niekro brothers grew up. Won most Gold Gloves (eight) ever by a second baseman. Holds major league records for most seasons leading league in assists (nine) and double plays (eight) and most double plays handled in a season (161) and career (1,706). Unsurprisingly, considered best ever at turning double play. Played entire career (1956–72) with Pirates. In 1960 Series handled 37 chances without error, batted .320, and in seventh game hit only home run ever to end a Series.

Ah, but how can one rush through a Mazeroski bio and still do him justice? For one thing, there was his *offense*. He will always be best known for that climactic homer, which some historians call the pinnacle of baseball history. It not only closed out the most exciting finale in any World Series, but it also climaxed baseball's best-played era. The next year the American

Bill Mazeroski of the Pittsburgh Pirates. *Pittsburgh Pirates*

League would expand from eight to 10 teams, and the National would follow suit in 1962. Post-Mazeroski, baseball began a steady decline into dilution.

Maz has mixed feelings about the homer because it overshadowed his estimable fielding. We see him now as he was then: muscles bulging out of that sleeveless jersey and black T-shirt as he threw over a sliding runner. "You have to stay in the line of fire when you turn that double play," says Mazeroski, who helped make Julio Cruz a fine second baseman while coaching at Seattle, made Tim Wallach into a fine third baseman while helping the Expos, and is now retired in Greensburg, Pa., outside of Pittsburgh. "If you're afraid, you'll never do the job. I always went right at the runner. If you cross the bag to the side, you take an extra step, give the runner two extra steps, and have to throw to first almost backward. It takes a special arm to make the double play throw. You have to release the ball quickly, with something on it.

"I was signed as a shortstop and switched to second in the minors. I pretty much learned the position myself—trial and error. I used only two or three gloves in my major league career. I'd break in one in practice and use my main one in games. Some guys have a new glove every year; you can't get the feel that way. I also used a small glove. When you reached for the ball, it was there.

"It takes a lot of range and quickness to play second. That's why you don't see many home run hitters. My greatest play? To tell you the truth, I never gave it any thought. Didn't have much TV in those days."

Well, here's a play. With the Pirates holding a one-run lead over the Mets and New York's speedy Tommie Agee on second, Mazeroski ran down a grounder past first, fielded it near the right-field line, and made a turnaround, off-balance throw of some 120 feet to nip Agee at home. And here's another. The Pirates were up by a run in the ninth, with Astros on first and third and one out, when a high hopper was hit to shortstop Gene Alley. Making the only play possible, Alley threw to Mazeroski for the force. On the bench the Pirates leaned back, conceding the run and girding for extra innings. Seconds later they realized the game was over. Mazeroski had somehow thrown to first in time to complete the DP. "That was one of the best double plays I ever made," he said when reminded of it. "Everyone wound up on the ground. Alley fell down making the throw, I turned it with my feet in the air, and Donn Clendenon hit the ground stretching for the throw at first."

Teammates referred to Mazeroski as Tree Stump because he often kept his vulnerable left foot stationary on double plays. When a runner slid into him, they had to bring out a stretcher —for the runner. "I never got hurt, but I sent about 12 guys out," Mazeroski says. Another oddity. When a hard-hit ball would glance off his glove for a hit, Mazeroski would occasionally complain that he should have been given an error. "That was embarrassing," he'd say. "I should have had it."

Since the second baseman is the most important man on most double plays, finding the best DP combination is a relatively simple task. It was Maz and Gene Alley (from 1965 to 1970), followed by Maz and Dick Groat (1956–62). "They both fed the double play well, so I wouldn't want to pick one over the other," says Mazeroski. "Alley had great range and a great arm, Groat had those fine hands."

There's certainly no question about Tree Stump's place among second basemen. Mazeroski had the highest fielding effectiveness and leader index ratings of any middle infielder evaluated by Jim McMartin. He had the highest defensive rating of any player John Thorn and Pete Palmer analyzed in *The Hidden Game of Baseball*, and they studied every position but pitcher. (The only active player with a chance to catch Maz, says Thorn, is Ozzie Smith.) Mazeroski deserves to finish first in another category: defensive stars who have been unjustly omitted from the Hall of Fame.

7

Third Base: The Hottest Corner and the Hardest Caroms

Given the position's modern respectability, it's appropriate that two third basemen were the key figures in the key inning of the 1980 baseball season. The World Series was tied at two games apiece, with the Royals ahead 3-2 and three outs from winning Game 5. As Philadelphia third baseman Mike Schmidt led off the ninth, his Kansas City counterpart, George Brett, moved even with the bag. Schmidt had homered earlier in the game, but he had bunted safely the day before, and Brett was taking no chances. This time, however, Schmidt swung away and hit a hard shot to Brett's left that the diving third baseman knocked down but couldn't make a play on. Schmidt's single sparked a two-run inning that enabled the Phillies to win 4-3. They wrapped up the Series two days later.

As exciting as the Series was—six games, five decided by one or two runs—it was the Schmidt-Brett confrontation on a Sunday afternoon that epitomized the season: the two leading teams, the two best players, the best-played position.

Ah, third base—alias Thunder Alley, or, more commonly, the Hot Corner. It has had that moniker since a game in 1889 in which Brooklyn batters smashed seven line drives at Cincinnati's Hick Carpenter. The rarest of players—one of a dozen lefthanded third basemen in baseball history—Carpenter survived the barrage and set a gutsy example for future players. But for reasons that aren't entirely clear, only eight third basemen—the fewest for any position—have entered the Hall of

Kansas City's George Brett in action: getting set, taking a ground ball, touching third.
Matthew L. Kaplan

Fame. They are Jimmy Collins of the Boston Braves and Red Sox (in 1945); Pie Traynor, Pirates (1948); Frank (Home Run) Baker, Philadelphia A's and Yankees (1955); Judy Johnson of the Negro Leagues (1975); Fred Lindstrom, Giants, Pirates, Cubs, and Dodgers (1976); Eddie Mathews, Braves (1978); Brooks Robinson, Orioles (1983); and George Kell, Tigers (1983).

The position began being noticed, if not immortalized, in the 1960s and 1970s, when Ron Santo, Clete and Ken Boyer, Sal Bando, Aurelio Rodriguez, Bill Madlock, Ron Cey, Doug Rader, Graig Nettles, and Mike Schmidt, to name quite a few, gave career fielding leader Robinson (see profile at end of chapter) a strong supporting cast. And in 1981, four years after he'd retired, Robinson declared, "There are more good third basemen today than at any other time in history, and more good players at third than at any other position."

In the aftermath of the 1980 season, the best of these, of course, were Most Valuable Players Brett and Schmidt. Brett had just batted .390 and led the Royals to their first pennant. Schmidt had won his fifth consecutive Gold Glove, led the Na-

San Diego Padres

A pair of expert third basemen: San Diego's Graig Nettles, top, and the Phillies' Mike Schmidt. *Paul H. Roedig: Philadelphia Phillies*

tional League with 121 runs batted in and 48 homers, and been MVP of the Series as well.

The position remained strong well into the 1980s, thanks to other all-around performers. Buddy Bell, formerly of Texas and later with the Reds, has hit as high as .329 and been a Gold Glove performer despite the debilitating heat and bad-hop infield of Arlington Stadium. Cey of the Dodgers and Cubs has hit with power and fielded with great proficiency on natural turf. Nettles of the Yanks and Padres has been a home run champ and was the fielding star of the 1978 World Series. Madlock of the Rangers, Giants, Cubs, Pirates, and Dodgers won four batting titles while fielding bunts as well as anyone in the game. Boston's Wade Boggs won three batting titles in his first five seasons while considerably improving his fielding; indeed, in 1985 he led all AL third basemen with 486 chances. And Doug DeCinces of the Orioles and Angels has been a feared power hitter and proficient gloveman despite constant back trouble. "In terms of starting the 5-4-3 double play, Doug DeCinces is without a doubt the best I've ever seen at getting it to the second baseman," says California manager Gene Mauch.

Some of these worthies began to show their age in the mid-1980s. No matter. There were others who had established themselves, like Milwaukee's Paul Molitor, Minnesota's Gary Gaetti, St. Louis's Terry Pendleton, Montreal's Tim Wallach, and Toronto's platoon of Rance Mulliniks and Garth Iorg. And there were enough promising youngsters on the way up—Seattle's Jim Presley and San Francisco's Chris Brown, to name a couple —to suggest that the position would remain strong.

The thrills of third never slacken. There are few sights as crowd-pleasing as that of a third baseman diving flat-out to his left or right to stab a hard smash. More than any other player, a third baseman must be willing to leave his feet and be able to make spectacular plays routinely. Equally relished by baseball insiders is the play third basemen make on bunts and slow rollers—fielding the ball off-balance, perhaps barehanded, and throwing to first in one motion. In the '85 postseason, Brett and Pendleton brought crowds to their feet with a much rarer play— ranging behind third or down the left-field line to field balls and throw out runners at the plate.

Though Schmidt concedes that Nettles's ability to make great plays under pressure was unequaled, the Phillie has generally been considered the best recent third baseman. Schmidt was the man with peerless requisites: a good arm, fine hand-eye coordination, and excellent reflexes. But what separated him from the pack was a quality lacking in most other men at his position: speed. Schmidt, who, like most top third basemen and second basemen played shortstop before switching over, ranged as far afield as any infielder, cutting off grounders in the hole and running down pops for over-the-shoulder catches. "I'll tell you this about his range," says *Philadelphia Inquirer* baseball columnist Allen Lewis. "I once saw Schmidt go to his left and cut off a ball in the hole. As he was moving and throwing to second for a force, he saw that his throw would be off-line. It tipped off the second baseman's glove, and Schmidt never stopped moving. He ran down his own throw in right field."

Fast enough to bunt successfully and steal bases, Schmidt exploited his speed in the field. "I play way off the line and back in the outfield," he once said. "I like to spice up the position." Unlike most of his peers, who recoil at the myriad horrors of the position, Schmidt considers it easier than any position but left field. "It's do or die," he put it. "With the tough plays, you've got nothing to lose. Most of them aren't made because the ball's hit so hard. So I'm relaxed. Maybe that's why I make more hard plays than the others.

"It's an instinctive, reflex position. I don't think it requires a lot of practice. About all I do is spend some time catching the ball and putting it behind my back and between my legs to develop a feel. You have to learn to cradle the ball, to have a body so limp the ball doesn't bounce too far when it hits you. And, of course, you have to enjoy playing out there."

Brett, an excellent clutch fielder who has overcome throwing deficiencies, is quick to agree. "When I came up," he says, "I never wanted to have a ball hit to me. Now I want 'em all the time."

The low regard in which previous generations held third is no longer evident, and that's as it should be. True, third basemen are recruited primarily to be power hitters in the middle of the lineup. True, a third baseman is less important to a team's defense than the up-the-middle positions. But the famous putdown by Hall of Fame second baseman Frankie Frisch rings hollow today. "There's nothing tough about playing third," he said. "All a guy needs is a strong arm and a strong chest."

To be frank, Frankie, a third baseman must be deft enough to field bunts and dribblers on the run and throw in one fluid motion; agile enough to react to hard-hit balls to his left and right; and fearless enough to take direct shots off his body. "You don't see many muscle-bound third basemen," says Bell. Nor many fainthearted ones. "When you reach the point where you're too slow to get out of the way," says Detroit's Tom Brookens, "it's time to quit." He's kidding, of course. A fielder who plays "matador" defense won't last long; at third you take your lumps and learn to love them.

"You don't think about getting hit by batted balls," says Brett, "any more than getting hit by pitched ones." Nonetheless, a third baseman's pain threshold is only so high. "Maybe that's why there are so few of them in the Hall," says Larry Parrish, who moved from third to the outfield in midcareer. "It's such a demanding position that few can hit with power and field well over a long career." Brooks Robinson's 23-year stint (1955–77) is the exception. Among the good third basemen who missed being elected to the Hall, Ken Keltner played 100 or more games in just 10 seasons. Al Rosen and Billy Cox seven each. More recently, back troubles forced Minnesota's John Castino, who came up as a third baseman, to cut short a promising career;[1] LA's Pedro Guerrero found he couldn't field the position and hit well at the same time and was sent to left, and Atlanta's Bob Horner has had shortened seasons because of constant wrist problems. The plethora of good third basemen in the early 1980s is perhaps the ultimate tribute to a hardy breed of men.

What makes for a good third baseman? Schmidt notwithstanding, speed isn't essential. Even if a third baseman is slow, he can compensate with fast reactions, sound baseball instincts, and aggressiveness. The position's most overrated attribute—Frisch notwithstanding—is a strong arm. Robinson had a middling arm but a lightning release. The most overrated statistic is errors, the most underrated, chances. In 1974 Robinson was awarded the Gold Glove over Milwaukee's Don Money, although Money had fewer errors (five to 18) and a higher fielding percentage (.989 to .967). But Robinson accepted 543 chances to Money's 472, and the voting wasn't close.

Third basemen can't agree on their most difficult play. A drive down the line, some say. "A two-hopper," says Nettles. "You can't go in or back, and you don't get any perspective on the ball." Most third basemen fear the surprise bunt. "You have

1. Castino should forever be remembered for a play he made in 1983. When a Metrodome grounder bounced over his head, he turned around and caught it facing left field. Then he wheeled, leaped, and threw in one motion to nip the Rangers' speedy George Wright at first.

National Baseball Library

to field it one-handed because you're moving at top speed," says Robinson. "If you field the ball with your left foot forward, you can throw right away, but it's awkward to bend down with your right foot forward. I always used a little stutter-step to get the left foot in front." Even an expected sacrifice bunt can be tough, especially if there are runners on first and second. Then the third baseman must instantly decide whether to retreat for third or field the ball himself. "The toughest play is a swinging bunt," argues Bell, referring to the slow roller that comes off a full swing and catches the fielder unaware.

Thus, instinct wins out over intelligence. "Next to the catcher, the third baseman has to be the dumbest guy out there," says

You can get a lot of votes for either Pie Traynor, longtime Pittsburgh Pirates star, left, or Clete Boyer, New York Yankees, above, as the best-fielding third baseman ever. *New York Yankees*

former Seattle third baseman Dave Edler. "You can't have many brains to take those shots every day." Parrish prefers the word flaky. "A guy can't be afraid to move up on the ball," said Eddie Mathews, whose backhand stab ended the 1957 World Series, "or play in on Ralph Kiner when a line drive could kill you. The third baseman has to be a guy who's right in there on the field or in a fight." Many is the shortstop or second baseman who has moved to third expecting a vacation from the bruises they'd suffered getting hit by baserunners breaking up double plays; few are the switchees who survived the transition with-

out getting bruised from head to toe by hard shots off the bat.
Perhaps the ultimate glory cum indignity for a third baseman
came in 1948 when George Kell had his jaw broken by a Joe
DiMaggio smash. Reacting instinctively, Kell picked up the
ball, crawled to third for the force out, and then fainted. Physi-
cally, the three most bruising positions are catcher, third, and
second.

Third basemen are survivors—in life if not in baseball. According to a study by the Metropolitan Life Insurance Company, third basemen live longer than other players. On the
other hand, they have less time to react to batted balls than
anyone else. Therefore, third basemen must position themselves
for hitters more precisely. "I've studied the position inside out,"
says Schmidt. "A guy's cheating himself and his teammates if he
doesn't take advantage of that knowledge."

The most celebrated defensive third basemen of all time
were Traynor, Robinson, and Clete Boyer. Traynor was an excellent batter who hit .320 from 1920 to 1937, but his defense was
particularly notable in an era when third basemen were considered fixtures rather than fielders. "He was a big, rangy guy
who took a bent-over stance with his hands on the ground,"
said late Hall of Fame pitcher Burleigh Grimes, Traynor's teammate in 1928, '29, and '34. "He was the first player I ever saw
cross over and backhand balls hit down the line; before Pie,
they were all doubles." Traynor was so dedicated that if he
made an error in a game, he would stay for an hour afterward
taking grounders. And that's not just another baseball legend.

Boyer, who played for the Kansas City A's, the Yankees, and
the Braves between 1955 and 1971, is often overlooked because
of his .242 lifetime average. "He'd start extremely low, like a
catcher, and then dive," says Woody Woodward, who played
with him in Atlanta. Says Boyer, "Even when we took infield
practice, I knew people were watching me. Guys from the other
team. Fans. I was on stage. I loved it. No distraction bothered
me. A third baseman has got to be like that, loaded with confidence." No less an authority than Robinson calls Boyer the best
third baseman he ever played against.

Sal Bando, who played for the A's and Brewers, underscores a
third baseman's importance to his team. "One advantage of a
good third baseman is that he can turn a double down the line
into an out." In 1941 Cleveland's Ken Keltner made two such
stops in one game to end Joe DiMaggio's 56-game hitting streak.
"That's a big difference," says Bando. "It can turn a game around

for a pitcher." As L.A.'s Junior Gilliam did for Sandy Koufax in the 1965 Series finale. Or it can turn a Series around for a team. With the Dodgers leading the Yankees two games to none in 1978, Nettles keyed a 5-1 Yankee win by robbing batters of at least five hits and perhaps as many as seven runs. The Yankees went on to win the Series four games to two. A year later, Robinson's successor, Doug DeCinces, finished off the Angels in the American League playoffs. Preserving a 3-0 Oriole lead in the fourth and final game, DeCinces dived across the bag to spear Jim Anderson's vicious one-hopper with the bases loaded, hooked the bag with his foot, scrambled to his feet, and fired to first to complete an inning-ending double play. As Robinson himself conceded from the Oriole broadcasting booth, the play was downright Brooksian.

BROOKS ROBINSON

Was there ever a man, a position, and an event better suited for each other than Baltimore's Brooks Robinson, third base, and the 1970 World Series?

Game One: Robinson makes three excellent plays, the best being his backhand stop of Lee May's smash. Robinson recovers it in foul ground 25 feet in back of third and throws out May at first.

Game Two: In the first inning Robinson dives to grab Bobby Tolan's smash and turns it into a force play. With another diving stab, he turns May's drive into a third-inning double play.

Game Three: In the first Robinson leaps for Tony Perez's high hopper, steps on third for a force, and throws to first for a DP. In the second he grabs Tommy Helms's swinging bunt barehanded and throws to first in one motion. In the sixth Robinson demonstrates his versatility by going to his left, diving, and stabbing Johnny Bench's liner.

Game Five: As the Orioles win the Series, Robinson sews up the Most Valuable Player award with another backhand stab of a Bench line drive.

Robinson had run the full gamut of third base expertise: backhanding the ball, turning and throwing to first while crossing into foul territory, scooping up a roller barehanded, and diving to his left for liners. His fielding was so spectacular it overshadowed his Series batting average of .429. "Brooks couldn't believe what a showcase the 1970 Series was for his fielding," said his shortstop, Mark Belanger.

No one who saw it will ever forget Brooks Robinson's performance at third base for the Baltimore Orioles in the 1970 World Series against the Cincinnati Reds. *Baltimore Orioles*

In a sense, the same could be said for Robinson's entire career. Everyone remembers his fielding; who remembers his 268 homers and 2,848 hits? But that's as it should be. The other six Hall of Fame third basemen got there primarily because of their hitting. As tough a fielding position as third deserves a Famer known for his fielding. Robinson is it.

Variously known as Hoover, the Human Vacuum Cleaner, and Mr. Impossible, Robinson won 16 Gold Gloves in 23 years and retired with a fielding percentage of .971, highest ever for his position. He was the quintessential gloveman. Indeed, he kept three of them in various stages of suppleness and with him at all times. Robinson did everything lefthanded except play baseball. "My glove hand is my better one," he said. "Maybe that's why I had such good reflexes with it." As the late umpire Ed Hurley said of Robinson, "He plays like he came down from a higher league." Pie Traynor, who lived until 1972, called Robinson "the best I've ever seen."

Paunchy and slouching, Brooks didn't look like the position's textbook toughie. But he had a way of making the most of what he had—or maybe making more than he appeared to have. He had very little speed or arm strength but excellent reflexes and anticipation. "What made Brooks a good third baseman," says Brett, "was that he charged everything. He reacted as the ball was coming off the bat, sometimes as it was coming *to* the bat." And some old-timers swear Robinson was the first third baseman they ever saw dive for the ball. "When I was playing with Brooks," says Belanger, "I was able to move two steps to my left and take away a lot of hits up the middle. That's what a good third baseman will do for you."

"I prefer third base," says Boston's Wade Boggs, "because it's a glamour position." Well, Robinson made it that way. That's the ultimate tribute to the ultimate third baseman.

8

Shortstop: The Athlete

Baseball is a game of interlocking triangles. You can see them out there: short, second, and first, the old double play combination; catcher, first, and left, the positions where you don't run or react much; third, catcher, and right, or Arms and the Men. But there's no baseball trinity quite as holy as pitcher, shortstop, and centerfielder. They're the confident kids who like the action and relish the responsibility. They're in the center of things: the centerfielder in the center of the outfield, the shortstop in the center of the infield, the pitcher in the center of the game.

Of these three glamour positions, the shortstop makes the toughest plays by far. Let Frank White have his way about the empirical importance of second base, the shortstop is easily the best athlete. Any all-star fielding lineup is filled with fine ex-shortstops. Mike Schmidt shifted from short to third, White and Bill Mazeroski from short to second, Hank Aaron, Carl Yastrzemski, Mickey Mantle, Roberto Clemente, and Pete Reiser from short to the outfield. But one rarely shifts from elsewhere to short.[1] "Look at Keith Hernandez," says baseball historian John Thorn. "Best first baseman I've ever seen—he makes Gil Hodges look like Zeke Bonura. But Hernandez could never play short. He doesn't have the range."

The shortstop has come a long way: from not existing at all in baseball's infancy, to the paradigm of the "good-field, no-hit" player, to his present position of preeminence. And he has never been as proudly preeminent as he is today. Quite simply, there have never been as many good shortstops as there have been playing in the 1980s.

---

1. The most notable exception was Detroit's Mickey Stanley, who was switched from center to short late in the season and helped the Tigers win the 1968 World Series.

One reason, of all things, is artificial turf. Despite its well-documented harm to the fielding of batted balls, turf has produced shortstops who can throw better than ever. The shortstop of the '80s has to play deeper on the quick carpets and needs a better arm to make those critical throws from the hole—plays that may be the difference between a double play and a two-men-on situation.[2] All of which incidentally may attract bigger men more likely to hit homers. Of the 14 shortstops in the Hall of Fame, none stood six feet tall or hit more than 170 home runs (Ernie Banks was installed as a first baseman). But consider the premier all-around shortstops of the 1980s: 6'4" Cal Ripken, Jr., 6' Robin Yount (before shoulder trouble forced him to switch to the outfield), and 6' Alan Trammell, all of whom can hit as well as they field.

Most shortstops are still short, but longer than ever on skills. An extraordinary influx of Hispanic middle infielders, mostly from the Dominican Republic, has given the position unprecedented depth. Spanish-speaking players started trickling in during the 1950s; now they're coming in a steady stream. Unlike Ripken and Company, they don't stand tall or hit for much distance. They atone with gymnastic dexterity—a useful trait when balls race through turf infields—and their slashing swings make many of them offensive threats as well.

The Dominican phenomenon is based on two factors: sugar and poverty. Sugar mills organize excellent baseball programs, and one of the few escapes from this impoverished country is professional baseball. Being generally smaller than Americans, even large Dominicans tend to congregate in the middle-infield positions, and they especially wind up at short because of their exceptional dexterity.

Well, a shortstop *has* to be dexterous. It's not enough that he has more balls hit to him than anyone else on the field. It's not enough that he's invariably the captain of the infield. Sometimes the shortstop feels as if he is the whole team. "One time, when I was playing shortstop with the White Sox, I had to call every pitch for a rookie catcher," says Kansas City utilityman Greg Pryor. "I'd get the signal from the pitching coach and re-

2. Indeed, we should pause over just how long those throws are. In the 1970 World Series, Cincinnati's Dave Concepcion noticed Baltimore third baseman Brooks Robinson unintentionally bounce a throw to first off the turf at Riverfront Stadium. Suddenly it occurred to Concepcion that he had been wasting his arm trying to throw all the way from deep short to first. Suffering elbow trouble the next season, Concepcion decided to intentionally bounce his long throws on turf fields, and a new art form was born.

He could play shortstop just as well as he could hit, and Honus Wagner won eight National League batting championships for the Pittsburgh Pirates between 1900 and 1911. *National Baseball Library*

lay it to the catcher, who called it for the pitcher. Besides four different signals for the catcher, I had to tell the second baseman who'd cover the bag on a steal or hit-and-run, the third baseman when a breaking ball was coming, and the pitcher who'd cover second on a hit back to him. It was the most taxing job I ever had. A couple of times I forgot to look over to the pitching coach. The catcher thought he saw me make a sign and called the pitch. Boy, were they yelling at me from the dugout!"

"The shortstop has to be more acrobatic than anyone else,"

says Chicago Cubs manager Gene Michael, a career shortstop. "He needs a quicker release because he has a longer throw from the hole." And he needs quicker feet to hold his position and then skitter to second to take a throw or to the outfield to handle relays.

"There's not much room for error at short," says Mark Belanger, the premier shortstop of the 1970s at Baltimore. "Any time you bobble or hesitate, the runner is probably going to be safe. That's not true at third, second, or first." Most players at those other positions won't argue the point. Says Pittsburgh's second base great Mazeroski, who has a beautiful knack for stating simple truths, "Shortstop is the toughest infield position because it has the longest throw."

Shortstop is as much of an art form as a pure athletic skill. Arm strength, for one, can be overrated. Players with cannons for arms frequently overthrow; most shortstops say the release is more important. It's also commonly believed that the play in the hole is far and away the toughest one a shortstop has to make. Actually, some shortstops prefer that play to the one behind second, in which they must throw right while moving left. This play is not only difficult but painful. Says Rick Burleson, crippled the latter part of his career with rotator cuff trouble: "When I have to make that throw with my body open and off-balance, my shoulder feels the strain more than at any other time." Finally, people have the same unfortunate tendency analyzing shortstop as second: to overrate flashy play. How does that square with the performance of Baltimore's mechanical man, Cal Ripken, Jr.? Ripken anticipates well and breaks for the ball the instant it leaves the bat. In 1985 he finished second in the American League to Toronto's Tony Fernandez in assists (478 to 474) while committing four fewer errors (30 to 26) and leading the league with 123 double plays. He was the best defensive shortstop outside of Ozzie Smith (see profile at the end of this chapter).

The shortstops of yore usually played like Ripken. Hall of Famer Lou Boudreau had to tape his sore feet before games, but his hands couldn't have been healthier. He had the highest shortstop ratings recorded by Jim McMartin in his noted 1983 statistical survey on middle infielders. Belanger wasn't flashy. Nor were Gene Alley, Phil Rizzuto,[3] Roy Smalley, Marty Marion, Luke Appling, Roy McMillan, Ron Hansen, or Pee Wee

3. Although he once caught a blooper barehanded to save a win.

National Baseball Library

Baltimore shortstops have long been among the game's best. Mark Belanger,
top, spears a line drive; Cal Ripken, Jr., fires to first to complete a double
play against the Chicago White Sox as Julio Cruz begins his slide, while
Lenn Sakata looks on. *Baltimore Orioles*

Reese. Not only was Honus Wagner anything but flashy, he could have coined the term "winning ugly" that was later used to describe the 1983 White Sox. When Wagner threw to first, it was said, he threw not only the ball, but chunks of dirt and grass too. The quintessential down-to-earth player is Larry Bowa, who set a National League shortstop's longevity record when he played his 2,154th and last game in 1985. Bowa had very limited range. He also made very few errors. When he retired, he had the highest fielding percentage of any shortstop past or present: .9796. Given a choice between the flashy player and the one who makes the basic plays, most managers will not hesitate to choose the latter.

"I see too many 14-to-16-year-olds who haven't mastered the basics: watch the ball, get to it, set your body, throw," says AL leader Belanger (.9768). But it's possible to oversimplify the flash-vs.-form controversy. The shortstops coming out of the Caribbean seem to have mastered both. Many of these athletes were brought up on fields so poor that if they lowered their body to catch two-handed, they'd risk losing their teeth. In "the Dominican," as the country is called in baseball circles, kids improve their reflexes by catching rubber balls fired off walls. In Colombia, Jackie Gutierrez played a game with a stick, a plastic ball, and six infielders; only grounders were permitted. White Sox' shortstop Ozzie Guillen, the 1985 American League Rookie of the Year, played a Venezuelan game called *pelota de goma* in which kids batted and caught hard rubber balls with their hands. In 1985 Guillen led all American League shortstops with a .980 fielding percentage while committing only 12 errors in 150 games. Guillen is an extraordinarily relaxed performer—"free on the field," as he puts it—who takes most routine grounders two-handed but warms up one-handed. He claims one-handed practice strengthens his glove hand; he claims further that it makes him stronger on plays where he has no choice but to use one hand; and he claims he has better body control one-handed. No one fields one-handed more than Ozzie Smith. The one-handed catch has swept the outfield; the one-handed fielder is gaining among shortstops.

What isn't likely to change is the role of the thinking man's shortstop. It's not enough to play the position reflexively; one must also play it reflectively. Because he didn't know the hitters in 1985, Guillen ran up 614 chances and 80 double plays to Ripken's 786 and 123. In time Guillen will play his position with the sophistication of an Ozzie Smith. "I try to know the hitters, but I try not to cheat too much one way or another when I'm positioning myself," says Smith. "The pitchers don't always throw the ball where the catcher calls for it, and a lot of hitters can move the ball around the park. You also have to consider speed. Against a guy like Tim Raines, you have to cheat in and up the middle. If he hits it in the hole, he'll beat it out anyway."

A shortstop is a little like a catcher in that he has to be so durable," says Kansas City manager Dick Howser. "He has to be prepared to play 150 games a year, and he has to want to. That's why I liked it when Guillen said in his rookie season that he'd be happy to play winter ball. I also like the fact that he doesn't mope. You make a lot of mistakes at shortstop; the important thing is to be able to come back."

It's the nature of shortstop that you can look good and bad on the same play. Don Buddin, the Red Sox' error-prone shortstop of the late 1950s and early 1960s, all but patented a play. He'd go deep in the hole, make a spectacular backhand stop, and throw the ball into the stands. It's the nature of shortstop that you can make history with wondrous and woeful play in the same year. In 1925 Roger Peckinpaugh of the Senators was named the American League's Most Valuable Player. In the World Series he committed a record eight errors. It's the nature of shortstop that your errors can mark you and even your kin for life. On September 13, 1942, Cub shortstop Len Merullo booted four plays in one inning. That morning his wife had given birth to a son. A sportswriter nicknamed the boy Boots Merullo.

All this fuss is being made over a position that originally didn't exist. Before 1845, baseball games were generally limited to eight men on a side, modeled as they were after that eight-man British game, rounders. There was no shortstop. In 1845 a New York Knickerbocker player named D. L. Adams inserted himself as a ninth man and accounted for the one position change in baseball history.

To this day, no one is certain where the name shortstop came from. Possibly from the cricket "short fielder," since the earliest shortstops were kind of short outfielders. They acted as relay men, the better to get the small, light ball in use at the time back into the infield. In 1856, when a heavier ball came into use, the Brooklyn Atlantics' 5'3" Dickey Pearce, who also invented the bunt, became the first shortstop to play in the infield. Afterward, all teams used the infield shortstop, but not uniformly. At times the shortstop played behind the pitcher; a free spirit, he could roam anywhere. But he always played inside the baselines. It wasn't until the mid-1860s that George Wright situated himself at the farthest reaches of the infield. Wright revolutionized the position. Suddenly, the once-nonexistent shortstop was the premier defensive player on the team, the man with the arm, the range, and the glove (well, shortstops didn't start using gloves for another two decades, but you get the idea). The shortstop could hit too.

Though Pearce had little power, he hit for a respectable average by bunting. In his time the bunt was patterned after the cricket hit; it had to bounce only once in fair territory to be considered a fair ball—that is, until the current fair-foul rule was instituted in 1877. People know Pete Rose tied Wee Willie Keeler's record by hitting in 44 consecutive games. Well, Keeler had broken a record of 42 straight set by Bill Dahlen, a turn-of-the-century shortstop. Jack Glasscock, who played from 1880 to 1895 and is considered the first outstanding shortstop, led the league in hitting with a .336 average in 1890. Even the supposed prototype of a weak-hitting shortstop, the immortal Rabbit Maranville, had 2,605 hits to go with his .258 lifetime average.

Shortstops didn't become known as weak hitters until Babe Ruth and the lively ball popularized the homer and revolutionized offense in the 1920s. The thinking, apparently, was: anyone can hit now, so let's give the most important position to a specialist in fielding. In time field was about all the shortstop did.[4] "If we could hit, we'd be playing somewhere else," says Dal Maxvill, who batted .217 but lasted 14 seasons because of his crack glove work. "If you had to have one trait, it was not to carry your offensive shortcomings onto the field when you played defense."[5]

Shortstops began playing especially skilled defense after World War II. First, gloves improved to the point where they could field one-handed. Then came the greatest player pool in the history of the position. A Venezuelan, Chico Carrasquel, joined the White Sox in 1950 and opened the gates for flashy

4. With some notable exceptions like Joe Cronin, Luke Appling, Lou Boudreau, and Arky Vaughan.

5. The prototype of the good-field, no-hit shortstop may have been the late Ray Oyler. When he was playing for the Tigers in 1965–68, he ran into the Detroit bullpen to make a diving catch, coming to rest on the warmup mound. Starting pitcher Earl Wilson was properly grateful. "I want that man in the lineup when I pitch," he said. "I'll hit for him."

Hispanic shortstops. His countryman, Luis Aparicio, succeeded him with the 1956 White Sox and took the art a step further. The most versatile shortstop to date, Aparicio had 2,677 career hits, virtually reintroduced the stolen base to baseball, and set major league records for his position in chances (12,564), assists (8,016), and games (2,581). About all Aparicio couldn't do was grow. He was 5'9". Then they installed artificial turf at the Astrodome in 1966 and ushered in the day of the longstop.

Mark Belanger, the premier shortstop of the 1970s, may have sensed times were changing the day he first saw Aparicio, the best shortstop of the 1960s. "When the Orioles signed me in 1962, they brought me to a game against the White Sox in which Aparicio went in the hole, backhanded the ball, jumped, and threw out the runner at first. I said, 'I'll never be able to do that.' They said, 'Oh, yes, you will.'"

And he did. Aparicio had adjusted to the faster fields by discarding the stubby gloves shortstops had used for years in favor of a mitt so large it resembles a jai alai basket. Belanger knew that being a smooth fielder wouldn't be enough. Rocking forward as the pitcher delivered the ball, he stretched his praying mantis arms and legs and 6'1" height for all they were worth, and developed one of the quickest releases ever seen.

"I always seemed to field my best against Lou Piniella and Frank Robinson," he says. "I fielded a ball Piniella hit on the grass, fell down, and still got up to throw him out. Against Robby I took a ball up the middle, made a 360-degree turn, and threw to Bobby Grich at second to start a double play."

These plays were among the highlights of Belanger's career. The glamour shortstop of the 1990s may make them routinely.

OZZIE SMITH

How good a shortstop is Ozzie Smith? Forget about all those Wizard of Aahs moves he stole from other sports: the sprawl saves and behind-the-back passes and reverse pivots and high hurdles. Just consider the kind of moves Ozzie Smith makes when no one is watching.

St. Louis first baseman Jack Clark was throwing warmup grounders to him one afternoon when Smith noticed that a balloon was arriving from his left as the ball was approaching from straight ahead. Ball and balloon continued to converge until it seemed inevitable that Smith would have to choose one or the other. Instead, in a sleight-of-hand maneuver that would have impressed Houdini, Smith reached out with his glove and batted away the balloon at almost precisely the moment he caught the ball.

"You saw that?" he exclaimed later, delighted that someone had shared in the magical moment. "I have good peripheral vision. Sometimes I can almost *hear* something approach from the side. Well, I saw the balloon out of the corner of my eye. I kept thinking it would go behind me until the moment when I flicked it away and caught the grounder. Maybe the balloon was a message. Maybe I should have popped it."

Will anyone ever pop Ozzie Smith's balloon? By the time he was 25, he had already established himself as the best player at baseball's toughest fielding position. He holds the record for most assists in one season—621 when he was a San Diego Padre in 1980. At 5'11", 150 pounds, he has the musculature of a gymnast; he's so acrobatic he was known for a cartwheel and back flip while running to his position in Busch Stadium on opening day and before big games. How do we love his fielding plays? Let us count the ways:

In 1978, Smith's first full season, Atlanta's Jeff Burroughs hit the grounder that made Smith famous when he dived, then reached behind himself to barehand the ball on an errant hop. Smith's play made all the highlight films, and his name instantly became known. People assumed he had been both good and lucky. What they didn't realize was that Smith had carefully prepared himself for just such an opportunity. "When I was a little kid, I used to throw a ball in the air and try to catch it with my eyes closed," Ozzie says. "There are a lot of times— say, when you're diving or fielding a bad hop—where you can't actually see the ball. Feeling is very important."

With the score tied 1-1, one out in the last of the seventeenth inning, and an Astro runner on third in a 1983 game, Smith went into the hole for a hard grounder by Alan Ashby. It was plainly a hopeless situation. Either the ball would go through, or Smith would field it too late to make the play at home. In any case, the winning run would score. Wrong. Smith took a couple of quick steps to his right, dived, speared the ball, and rose in virtually the same motion. Then he checked the runner back to third and threw out Ashby by 10 feet, after which Smith also retired the next batter. Galvanized, the Cardinals scored twice in the eighteenth to win 3-1. "Anyone can make a great play," Smith said. "I get special satisfaction from making one with a game on the line."

On a 1984 play against the Cubs, Smith fielded a slowly hit

The St. Louis Cardinals' great Ozzie Smith takes infield practice. *Matthew L. Kaplan*

ball behind the mound and instinctively threw a 25-foot behind-the-back pass to second baseman Tom Herr for a force out. "Hey," Smith says he thought, "I've just created something."

But it's an impossible task to categorize all of Ozzie's great plays. Asked to cite one, Smith and two of his former fellow Cardinals, infield coach Hal Lanier and infielder Art Howe, mentioned a stop in the hole Ozzie had made off Montreal's Andre Dawson. Each had a different version: Smith that he went down on one knee, Lanier that he dived, Howe that the play occurred in St. Louis, not in Montreal, as the others had claimed. In all probability, Smith had made three such unforgettable plays on Dawson.

"He gets up like a cat," says Cincinnati's slick-fielding shortstop Dave Concepcion. Met first baseman Keith Hernandez, Ozzie's old teammate, says Smith's best moves are more subtle ones. "On double plays, when he was taking the ball from me or Tommy, he'd straddle the bag. When he knew which side the ball was coming to, he'd fake in the other direction and draw the runner's slide. Bill Madlock is the best I've ever seen at taking out the pivotman, but Ozzie left him in the dust."

"People think you have to be able to throw the ball through a brick wall," says Smith. "That's a myth. The important thing is get the guy out." Unorthodox to the core, Smith often one-hands balls or throws with both feet in the air. "I do it the way I feel most comfortable," he says. "I still concentrate on the basics—catch the ball, throw the ball—but that may mean diving or catching it off-balance." During batting practice Smith stands as close as 80 feet to the hitter to test his reflexes, and he works on backhanding balls and taking them off short hops. During games he stands deep in the hole, the better to pick off hard shots; he's still fast enough to run down slow rollers.

"I like to prepare myself for the element of surprise," he says. "I try to keep my weight evenly balanced so that I can move to my right or left. I move around to get into the flow of the game with the pitcher. When it's hard to get into the rhythm, I bend lower."

But don't judge Smith purely by logic or data. He's too elusive for that. He's the Wiz.

9

Fielder's Choice

Here's a potpourri of fielding gems:

One pitch: The Cardinals were leading the Royals 2-1 with one out in the fifth inning of the 1985 World Series opener when Willie McGee stepped in against KC's Danny Jackson. The Royals had decided to throw McGee low, off-speed pitches. With the count 1-2, however, Jackson and catcher Jim Sundberg wanted to waste a fastball outside the strike zone to set up the next pitch. The fastball made a sizzling sound like the fizz on a glass of ginger ale. Unfortunately, it hung tantalizingly in the strike zone. McGee hit the ball on a line deep to right-center.

Royal fans sensed disaster. McGee would undoubtedly reach third, Ozzie Smith would surely drive him in, and the Cardinals would have a two-run lead for mighty John Tudor. Fortunately, the nine men on the field were too busy to be despondent. Centerfielder Willie Wilson and rightfielder Darryl Motley converged on the ball. Leftfielder Lonnie Smith moved toward third in case of a rundown, and pitcher Jackson headed over to back up the throw there. Third baseman George Brett stood by his bag. Catcher Sundberg remained at home in case of an overthrow. First baseman Steve Balboni followed the runner toward second to take the throw there in case McGee retreated after a wide turn. Second baseman Frank White and shortstop Buddy Biancalana headed into center field for the relay.

The ball hit the base of the fence and bounced directly to Wilson. "Hit the cutoff man!" Motley yelled at him. Wilson wheeled and threw instinctively; he had no time to look first for White or Biancalana. On balls hit to right-center, the second baseman makes the relay, backed up by the shortstop. White and Biancalana had run well into the outfield. "Willie doesn't have a strong arm," says White, "and you don't want the throw to bounce. I ran out trying to align myself between Willie and

Kansas City Royals

National Baseball Library

Matthew L. Kaplan

Three Kansas City standouts: top, Willie Wilson; bottom left, Buddy Bian-calana, with glove held close to ground; and, right, Frank White, going back on a fly ball.

third. You have to have court awareness as in basketball, and you look over your shoulder to third as you run out." For his part, the trailing Biancalana had duties beyond grabbing the ball if White missed it. It was up to him to help White with his alignment and throwing decision. "Left, left, left!" or "Right, right, right" or "Run it in!" or "Cut and hold!" Biancalana might yell. Because there was bound to be a throw to third and White was aligning himself well, Biancalana simply shouted, "Third, third, third!"

Wilson's throw to White was perfect, and as Biancalana ducked, White turned and threw to third. Brett stood there motionless and impassive. Often a runner will look to the third baseman's eyes or body movement to decide whether to slide; Brett gave McGee no clue whatsoever. What he did give McGee was the ball. White's throw was on-line, Brett's tag was sure, and McGee was out trying to stretch a double: 8-4-5. It was the ultimate team play by the ultimate team playing.

Team defense turns on such subtleties as alignment and communication. "One reason we're such a good team defensively is the way Vince Coleman, Willie McGee, Tito Landrum, and I play the outfield," Cardinal rightfielder Andy Van Slyke said early in 1986. "We're constantly throwing guys out. Then"—he holds up both hands like a third-base coach signaling stop— "the runner doesn't take the extra base. Then maybe Ozzie [shortstop Ozzie Smith] or Tommy [second baseman Tommy Herr] throws someone out, or we get a double play, and we're out of the inning. That doesn't show up in the stats, but it's one of the reasons we're so tough."

It's amazing how well ballplayers concentrate in the field. Rarely does a player begin leaving the field when there are two outs; rarely does he stay on when there are three; rarely does he throw to the wrong base on a fielder's choice situation. From an early age players are taught to be aware of the count, the number of outs, and what to do if the ball is hit their way. "I think you're in trouble," says Cincinnati manager Pete Rose, "if you have to tell players to concentrate on the game."

Nonetheless, some concentrate better than others. "I look over to Willie Wilson," says Motley, "and I see him crouched with his hands on his knees even when the ball isn't being pitched. That helps me concentrate better myself." Any player will tell you that he concentrates better behind a fast-working pitcher: less chance for distraction. And even as consummate a player as George Brett didn't become a complete third base-man until he listened to some advice from utilityman Greg Pryor. Before the 1985 season Pryor told Brett he could concen-trate better by anticipating that every ball would be hit his way, instead of thinking about his next or last at-bat or looking up into the stands. Brett went on to win his first Gold Glove.

The pivotman gets most of the attention on the double play, and rightly so. He's the guy in the line of fire, and he's the player who must make both a putout and an assist for the play to work. No wonder former Yankee Bobby Richardson learned five different pivots while winning his five Gold Gloves.

However, it's wrong to think of the play solely in terms of the pivotman's difficult job. For one thing, his job is easier than it has ever been. These days the runner must be able to touch the base while sliding—a considerable improvement over the time in which he could chase the pivotman from here to Tierra del Fuego. In addition, many second basemen protect themselves with the bag or cross the base toward the infield side, while many runners slide directly into the base or slightly toward its outfield side.

So now it's time to consider his partners on the DP—the man who starts it and the man who finishes it. Be it a Doug DeCinces or an Ozzie Smith, the best left-side players at starting DPs get rid of the ball with all deliberate speed. Most of them will do so without taking a step; they'll just field and fire. On the right side of the infield, players like Charlie Neal, who is best remem-bered as a Dodger second baseman, and the righthanded first baseman Vic Power often fielded the ball backhanded, so that they were already facing second. And all fielders will try man-fully to hit the pivotman with a chest-high throw. Giant short-stop Alvin Dark spent a winter fretting about a throw he made just slightly off-line in the 1954 World Series.

In Game Two the Indians' Al Smith was on second and Bobby Avila on first when Rudy Regalado hit a one-out grounder to the right side. Dark fielded it smartly, then threw about a foot from where he was aiming in the center of second baseman Dave Williams's chest. Williams caught the ball to force Avila, but threw too late to first for the double play. Immediately, Dark began to worry that the next batter, the feared Vic Wertz, would homer and put the Indians ahead 4-3. Instead, Wertz was retired, and the Giants won 3-1 and went on to sweep the Series.

Dark wasn't satisfied. "I gave Dave the ball on his outside shoulder instead of his chest," Dark told Joe King of the *New York World-Telegram and Sun* the next spring. "It made all the difference between a double play he could have made and one he didn't. His throwing rhythm was ruined. The absolutely essential part of the double play is the first throw. The play is made or lost there. The target is about the size of the glove on the chest of the pivotman. He is a machine adjusted to receive the throw there. You cannot be far off target and give him much chance on a close play. When a pivotman throws wild to first he goes down for an error, but in most cases the error was caused by a poor first throw, which is not penalized."

More recently, pivotmen have learned to throw to first from wherever they receive the ball. That takes some pressure off the man who starts the DP, and puts more on the guy who ends it— usually the first baseman. The relay to first is invariably closer than it is on a single throw, 6-3, 5-3, or 4-3. Because the relay throw must be rushed, it's also likely to be inaccurate. More than ever, the first baseman must make a good stretch or scoop —or a good show to convince the umpire the batter is out.

The scoop is a well-recognized art form, and scooping toward the ball instead of giving with it the preferred practice. "It's easier to start down and lift up," says Keith Hernandez. If the throw is high enough but up the right-field line, many a first baseman is taught to touch the base with the toes of his left foot and stretch with his right foot for maximum extension, and do the reverse for a throw on the home plate side. Not Hernandez. "Look," he says. He puts his right foot on an imaginary base and stretches with his left foot and right glove hand. Now he reverses feet—and reaches a few inches farther. "I always have my left foot on the bag," he says. "It's more comfortable." The lesson: stretch with the foot on the glove-hand side.

First basemen frequently leave the bag an instant before they catch the throw. This technique must be used with care. "One thing you don't want to do is put an umpire on the spot," says Pete Rose. "On non-close and close plays you should take the throw the same way. You don't want to stand on the bag and hold the ball five seconds. I also don't think I leave the base that early. I give the umpire a good tag and then get off the base."

Says former umpire Ron Luciano, "They teach us to look at the bag and listen for the sound of the ball hitting the glove. Are you kidding? You're telling me you can hear the *pfft* of the

ball hitting a glove before 50,000 people in Yankee Stadium?
What you do on those plays is look at the bag and watch for
some movement of the feet as the first baseman stretches. A
guy can cheat a little and come off the bag before he gets the
ball. Mike Squires was the best I've ever seen at that. He was
especially good at doing it on balls in the dirt. You'd see him
make a tough scoop, and you'd give him the call. Then he'd say,
'Got you again, Ron.' But most of the time you should only
leave the bag early on a moderately close play. If you do on a
bang-bang play, you'll get a reputation, and the umpires will
think you're showing them up. It's like the guy who starts toward first on a 3-0 pitch: No way you're getting that one, buddy.
Watch Keith Hernandez on bang-bang plays, and he'll keep his
foot on the bag."

Actually, he only appears to. "I cheat a little on close plays,"
he says. "Ron Fairly [the former Dodger and Expo outfielder–
first baseman] taught me how to get off the bag ahead of the
throw, and do it in one fluid motion." Squires, the excellent
utility player who retired after the 1985 season, was equally
adept. "I'd get to the bag quickly," he says, "and as soon as the
ball hit the glove, I'd be off the base. I did that 99 percent of the
time. Once in a while, if the play was really close and a Willie
Wilson was running, I'd be 6 or 7 inches off the base when I
caught the ball. I'd pick my spot."

One of baseball's lingering problems is its official scoring. In
addition to tabulating stats and sending them to the league
office, scorers are often called upon to make judgment calls—
most notably, hits and errors. Scorers are usually baseball
writers. Because they must deal with players in the clubhouse
after making controversial calls, scorers are under heavy and
often successful pressure to take the path of least resistance.
Generally, that means ruling hits instead of errors on border-
line plays. In short, fielders are not being held to the highest
standards.

In recent years many metropolitan daily newspapers have
realized that their beat reporters can't cover the news and
make it simultaneously and have been removing them from
scoring duties. Unfortunately, their replacements have been reporters from suburban papers who may not travel with teams
and retired sportswriters with impaired vision and reflexes.
Scoring has never been worse.

The solution: baseball should hire a fifth umpire for each

crew. All umpires would be trained to keep score just as they are to make calls, and each crew member would score every fifth game. Umpires are used to making controversial decisions; presumably, they could stand up to players questioning their scoring calls too.

Baseball also might get around to adopting a long-overdue rule: the team error. As things stand, hits are generally awarded when a ball drops between two players. Since neither man tried for the ball and botched it, the scorer feels he has no choice but to award a hit. That's unfortunate, because the ball should have been caught. If there were a team error on the books, the decision would be simple. Team errors could also be given to throws by outfielders that went on-line to the base but caromed off a runner's back and allowed him to take an extra base. Currently, the outfielder is penalized for an accident of fate rather than a poor throw. The team error has been recommended but never adopted.

The baseball box score used to provide more information in a compact way than almost any known form of communication. Now it reads more and more like a crossword puzzle.

Until recently, boxes listed assists and putouts next to each player. This simple expedient was a key to understanding the game. "If you had a righthanded power pitcher and his second baseman was getting a lot of chances, you knew the pitcher was doing his job," says Paul MacFarlane, historian at *The Sporting News*. "If you have a sinkerball pitcher and his infielders are getting a lot of assists, he's doing his job too."

Alas, in 1964 the wire services decided to narrow the width and reduce the length of box scores. In a move that annoyed serious baseball fans everywhere, the Associated Press and United Press International dropped assists and putouts and the names of fielders involved in double plays and triple plays. "A box score is simply a list of fielders in a batting order," says MacFarlane. Today readers know little more than how those fielders performed as hitters.

Tricks of the trade: "When I'm in the field, I wear a batting glove on my left hand and put adhesive tape on the little finger and thumb," says utilityman Greg Pryor. "There are finger loops in the fielder's glove where you slip in your little finger and thumb, so the tape gives me a snug fit. The glove feels like an extension of my hand rather than a foreign object. It doesn't slip. That can be the difference between a ball getting away from you and an out."

Red Schoendienst, a Cardinal coach and former second baseman, was asked how he avoided getting spiked while making a tag. Schoendienst took the handle end of a bat and drew a base in the sand. "You straddle the base so you can go either way with the throw," he said, placing his right foot on the outside of the bag and his left foot on the inside. "The only parts of your body that are vulnerable are your left foot and glove hand. As the runner comes at you, you tag him and give with your glove and left foot. You won't get hurt that way.

"But the biggest thing about playing second or third or any other position is not being scared. You can always worry about being hit by a runner or a bad hop. As Pepper Martin used to say, you have to play this game with reckless abandon." (Martin was said to play with no protection under his uniform pants.)

You remember the hidden ball trick. Assuming the pitcher had the ball, the runner would wander innocently off base, only to be tagged out by an infielder. This ploy was used often in the nineteenth century; it isn't used much anymore because runners and coaches are too wise. Nonetheless, Boston second baseman Marty Barrett somehow pulled the trick twice on the Angels in 1985. "Aw, I knew he had it," said Bobby Grich, a victim. "I just had to go to the bathroom."

Then there's the hidden no-ball trick. The runner on first takes off with the pitch, the batter connects, and as the runner comes into second the shortstop or second baseman tags him with an empty glove. The runner slides. Meanwhile, the batter has singled to right or flied out. The sliding runner is either prevented from reaching third or doubled up. Kansas City shortstop Fred Patek worked this decoy play and helped his team win a playoff game in the late 1970s. Ozzie Smith decoys all the time. Fans rarely see the play; they're watching the ball.

Asked how he gets such a great jump on the ball from his position in center field, Willie Wilson said, "You look at the location of the pitch and the swing. Batters usually pull inside pitches and hit outside pitches to the opposite field, and they usually hit the ball far if they swing hard. I don't watch the batter, just the ball and the bat. When they take a big swing and just get a piece of the ball, that's when you take a step back and have to run in. That's when you get fooled."

*

Baseball is a game of small details and infinite care. Few understood this better than the late Jim Hegan, a Cleveland catcher in the 1940s and 50s. Hegan lasted 17 seasons despite a .228 career average and is considered by some to be the finest catcher of the last 40 years. Coaching for the Yankees in 1978, he spoke about baseball minutiae at spring training. His audience consisted of catcher Jerry Moses and Red Smith of *The New York Times*. Smith found Hegan throwing balls into the dirt for Moses to trap.

"'He wants to block a wild pitch and keep the ball in front of him,'" the coach explained. "'If his body is turned at an angle or if the mitt is, the ball can glance away and let runners advance. We don't want him to catch the wild pitch, just block it. He wants to be square on his knees with the mitt square between the knees and the meat hand behind the mitt.

"'Little things. You'd be surprised how many catchers don't know them. Like I ask them, on the double play that goes to the plate and then first base, what foot steps on the plate? The left foot does, and as you throw your stride takes you toward first so the man sliding home doesn't hit you. If the throw is off here to your left, then you have to shift and your chance for the double play is gone, anyway. . . .

"'Or when you chase a bunt or a topped ball out in front of the plate, how do you throw to first? Do you turn right and throw underhand, or do you pivot left? There are two ways to do anything and usually the most comfortable is the best. If you come out and pivot left, your arm will be in position to throw, and the overhand throw is easiest to handle. The throw from down here tends to veer off.

"'Usually the catcher has more time than he thinks, time enough to pivot left. Same when the runner is stealing second. If the pitcher doesn't let him get too big a jump, the catcher usually has plenty of time unless it's an exceptionally fast man. Most of these little things, the fans don't even think about.'"

An "outfielder's sky" is a baseball term for a background against which an outfielder can best see fly balls. The optimum outfielder's sky is dull, even gray—the ball stands out against it. Outfielders don't particularly like sunshine because they can lose balls in the glare; or clouds, because balls disappear coming in and out of them. Night light in outdoor stadiums is also uneven, and indoor light may be the worst of all. In Minnesota's Metrodome visiting players have complained that there's too little light in one part of the field and too much in another. In Seattle's Kingdome players have said that balls are fine coming off the bat but terrible in the overhead lights.

Getting down to earth, field conditions have long affected play. Artificial turf and varying heights of natural grass cause balls to skip or slow down through the outfield. For a long time groundskeepers have hardened infields for fast runners and softened them for the aged and infirm. At Anaheim Stadium and Wrigley Field in mid-1983 the infields had jungle-high grass and swamp-thick dirt. Playing infield for the Angels were Rod Carew, 37, Bobby Grich, 34, and Doug DeCinces, Tim Foli, and Rick Burleson, all 32. The left side of the Cub infield consisted of Larry Bowa, 37, and Ron Cey, 35. Both teams played considerably better on natural grass than ersatz green.

Lefthanded fielders are discriminated against in baseball, but understandably so. There has been only a handful of lefties who ever played third, short, or second. Righthanders at those positions can simply field the ball and throw to bases on their left; lefties must field, *pivot*, and throw. Only lefthanded Wee Willie Keeler, who "hit 'em where they ain't" at the turn of the century, was capable of playing where they ain't too. In his 19-year career, he played 44 games at third, 19 at second, and two at short.

But what about lefthanded catchers? The most recent of this rare breed are Dale Long of the 1958 Cubs and Mike Squires of the 1980 White Sox. Squires also played some third in 1983 and 1984 and pitched a third of an inning in 1984. "The idea that lefthanders can't catch is a fallacy," he says. "People told me it was because there were so many righthanded batters in the old days and a lefthanded catcher might hit them while throwing to second." But fully 45 percent of all everyday players bat left or switch-hit, and no one complains that righthanded catchers will hit *them*. The real reason is tradition and inertia.

"I can understand the problem with lefthanders playing third," says Squires. "I fielded a grounder, had to pivot 180 degrees before throwing to second, and we missed the double play by half a step. But lefthanders can play catcher because all the plays are right in front of them. On bunts, they can get the ball to first faster than righthanders, who have to pivot. There's no doubt that if a young lefthanded kid were brought up as a catcher, he could make it."

Speaking of playing where they ain't, one centerfielder reportedly caught a ball in foul territory. Johnny Mostil, who played center for the White Sox in the 1920s, was constantly covering for his leftfielder, Bibb Falk. On one afternoon in Nashville's Sulphur Dell park, which was about the size of your living room, Mostil noticed that Falk wasn't chasing a high, looping foul down the left-field line. According to the story, Mostil ran into foul territory, lunged into the stands, and made the catch.

Herb Caen of the *San Francisco Chronicle* reported a local bartender asking his customers the following question: What do Michael Jackson and the San Francisco Giants have in common? The answer: Both wear a glove on one hand for no apparent reason.

The Chicago Cubs wore gloves for a very apparent reason in a 1983 game against the Pirates. With two on and no outs, third baseman Ron Cey fielded Rick Rhoden's grounder, stepped on third for one out, and fired to second baseman Ryne Sandberg for another force, and Sandberg relayed to first baseman Bill Buckner to complete the triple play. The next time the Pirates batted, they went down on three pitches. That's a total of four pitches and six outs.

"These are the saddest of possible words: 'Tinker to Evers to Chance'"—Franklin P. Adams, *Baseball's Sad Lexicon*. Adams here immortalized the 1903–10 Cub double play combination of shortstop Joe Tinker, second baseman Johnny Evers, and first baseman Frank Chance. Actually, none of them ever participated in more than 73 twin killings in a season; 173 by a team are not uncommon today. However, modern revisionists who pooh-pooh the Cub combo miss the point. For one thing, their DP totals were bound to be low in the dead-ball era. And they were superb infielders and innovators who fully merited their places in the Hall of Fame.

They were a strange threesome—Tinker and Evers, who scarcely spoke to each other, and Chance, the "peerless leader" and manager, who in 1906 traded for third baseman Harry Steinfeldt, the forgotten man of the infield. The Cubs immediately won three straight pennants.

Evers, "a bundle of nerves with the best brain in baseball" according to sportswriter Hugh Fullerton, may have popularized the cutoff on double-steal situations with men on first and third. Not only would Evers rush behind the pitcher's mound to intercept the catcher's throw and halt the runner at third, he'd then feed the ball between his legs to Tinker to catch the runner coming into second. Tinker, Evers, and Chance also popularized the tactic now used by fielders on sacrifice situations. As the pitcher threw to the hitter, Chance charged in from first, Evers covered first, and Tinker moved to take care of second. The 3-6 force at second base from Chance to Tinker is what really made the threesome famous. Well, that and the poem.

Two of the best-known fielding glitches in World Series history were made by Fred Snodgrass of the 1912 Giants and Johnny Pesky of the 1946 Red Sox. When the Red Sox came from behind to score twice in the tenth and beat the Giants 3-2 in their 1912 finale, Snodgrass dropped Clyde Engle's leadoff fly. When the Cardinals scored the winning run in the eighth inning of the seventh game in 1946, Pesky supposedly allowed Enos Slaughter to score from first on a single by delaying before relaying the ball home. Neither Snodgrass nor Pesky deserves the rap.

It's true Snodgrass dropped Engle's fly. Snodgrass also made a spectacular catch off the next batter, Harry Hooper. Here's how Hooper described it to Lawrence Ritter in *The Glory of Their Times*:

"I was up next and I tried to bunt, but I fouled it off. On the next pitch I hit a line drive into left center that looked like a sure triple. Ninety-nine times out of a hundred no outfielder could possibly have come close to that ball. I don't know how, Snodgrass ran like the wind, and dang if he didn't catch it. I think he *outran* the ball. Robbed me of a sure triple.

"I saw Snodgrass a couple of years ago at a function in Los Angeles, and I reminded him of that catch.

"'Well, thank you,' he said, 'nobody ever mentions that catch to me. All they talk about is the muff.'"

The record should also show that Giant infielders subsequently misplayed Tris Speaker's foul pop, enabling him to stay at bat and knock in the tying run.

Pesky didn't allow Slaughter to score from first on a single. Slaughter scored on a *double* by Harry (The Hat) Walker. By the time the ball reached Pesky, there may have been no way to stop Slaughter, who had been running on the pitch.

*

All right, you've been titillated long enough. Herewith the greatest fielding play in baseball history. A hint: it was made by a player who didn't field a batted ball.

On September 23, 1908, the Giants apparently beat the Cubs on Al Bridwell's two-out, ninth-inning single to score Moose McCormick from third. However, Cub second baseman Johnny Evers noticed that Fred Merkle, the runner on first, hadn't bothered to touch second on the play and instead had run to the clubhouse in center. Evers procured a ball—it still isn't clear if he was holding the ball Bridwell hit—stepped on second to force Merkle, and appealed to umpire Hank O'Day.

Seventeen days earlier the Cubs had lost 1-0 to Pittsburgh, and Evers had claimed that the Pirates' young first baseman Warren Gill failed to touch second on the game-winning hit. Evers had been overruled by O'Day, but the arbiter had conceded he'd reconsider the next time. Once the field was cleared on September 23, O'Day relented, declared the game a 1-1 tie, and ordered it rescheduled if necessary to the pennant race on October 8.

As it happened, the Cubs and Giants finished the season tied for first place with 98-55 records. The Cubs won the rescheduled game 4-2, thus winning a pennant on Merkle's mistake and Evers's intelligence. Chicago's World Series victory over Detroit was actually considered an anticlimax.

For the rest of his career Merkle was known as Bonehead Merkle. A new English word—"boner," for pathetic performance—was born out of his baseball nickname. So consider Johnny Evers's heads-up play. It contributed to a pennant, a world championship, and a new word in the mother tongue. That's why this nonfielding play should be considered baseball's greatest moment in the field.

10

The Outfield

One does not think of outfields the way one thinks of infields. To begin with, there's no formalized outfield practice to compare with infield drills. Oh, sure, outfielders will take flies. The smart ones, like Boston's Dwight Evans, will always be simulating game situations; the smart fungo hitters, like California's Jimmie Reese, will hit flies that force fielders to run a little harder, stretch a little farther. Some teams will practice fielding base hits and making throws—right to third, center to home—complete with cutoff men. But there's a casual, almost voluntary quality to these drills. They're like extra-credit papers in English class.

That's the nature of the outfield. Rarely are outfields viewed as units. The three men in each assemblage seem to stand apart, patrolling their territories like lawman on the prairie. Or maybe the typical outfield should be viewed as a collection of animals: the centerfielder as roadrunner, the leftfielder as lead-footed buffalo, the rightfielder as powerful leopard. But a unit? Three of a kind? Not often.

Except, of course, the best outfields. From the immortal 1910–15 Red Sox threesome of Harry Hooper in right, Tris Speaker in center, and Duffy Lewis in left (see profile) to the modern pacesetters, the 1979–82 A's contingent of Tony Armas in right, Dwayne Murphy in center, and Rickey Henderson in left, outfielders have known each other like brothers and communicated like field commanders.

All great outfielders play alike. They stand as close to the infield as they dare, cognizant that most balls are hit in front of them, and confident enough to go back on balls hit over their heads. They field with their bodies in a position to throw and lined up toward the target. They have strong arms, fast feet, and quick reflexes. And, lately, they're starting to look alike too.

Oakland Athletics   *Oakland Athletics*

Matthew L. Kaplan

Top, left to right, the 1981 Oakland A's outfield: Ricky Hen-
derson, Dwayne Murphy, Tony Armas; below, left: Dane Iorg,
Kansas City; and right: the 1986 Boston Red Sox outfield:
Jim Rice, Tony Armas, Dwight Evans.

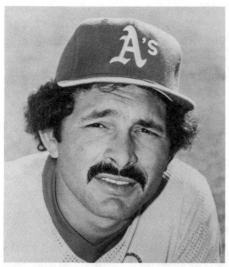

Oakland Athletics

Matthew L. Kaplan

Artificial turf has put a premium on speed, and uniform field dimensions have reduced extra-long throws, so some of the best modern outfields—the A's of the early-1980s, the Cardinals of the mid-1980s—are made up of natural centerfielders.

"We don't say 'I got it,'" Henderson said when he was with the A's. "We say, 'I got it, I got it, I got it.'" Unofficial outfield captain Murphy, unlike most centerfielders, sat in on pitcher's meetings, the better to know how batters were being worked, the better to reposition his fielders accordingly. The later the game, the more the A's played hitters to pull, reasoning that their pitchers were tiring. The A's outfielders threw hard between innings, Murphy and Armas playing catch and Henderson tossing to a bullpen catcher. "They're stretching their arms," A's coach Charlie Metro told *Sports Illustrated*'s Ron Fimrite. "They're throwing seriously, like a pitcher in the bullpen. They're getting in more throws between innings than the average outfielders. They're keeping warm for that one big throw."

In 1981, their peak year as a threesome, Armas, Murphy, and Henderson made many such throws. Though opposing runners were increasingly reluctant to take extra bases against them, they still had more assists (21) than errors (14). There was little hitting the ball up the gaps against the A's, because all three were speedsters who had started as centerfielders. Henderson led the American League in total chances with 341—virtually unprecedented for a leftfielder—and Murphy was second with 337. Both won Gold Gloves, and Armas might have added a third if Evans hadn't built up a superior reputation in his 10 previous years to Armas's six.

The Oakland Three contributed mightily to the A's division title. During the "second season" of that strike year, a research scientist named Dick Cramer tracked fly balls hit by the A's and their opponents that traveled at least 160 feet and didn't clear the fence. He discovered that 52.7 percent of the balls hit by A's dropped for hits, but only 44.8 percent of those hit by other teams did. Cramer calculated that with an average outfield the A's would have lost an additional 15 games—and their title.

It's unusual for outfields to contribute so much for the simple reason that they don't last long as units. Oh, there was the famous Yankee threesome of Bob Meusel in left, Earle Combs in center, and Babe Ruth in right during the mid-to-late 1920s, but they were better known for their bats than gloves. Another Yankee outfield—Charlie Keller, Joe DiMaggio, and Tommy

Henrich—only lasted three years. The Dodgers' Andy Pafko, Duke Snider, and Carl Furillo survived less than two, the Orioles' Don Buford, Paul Blair, and Frank Robinson less than three. The Red Sox' heralded unit of 1975–80 wasn't quite pure. If Evans was a fixture in right and Fred Lynn in center, Carl Yastrzemski and Jim Rice shared left. A celebrated seven-year unit, Davy Jones, Sam Crawford, and Ty Cobb of the 1906–12 Tigers, wasn't pure either, since Jones played sporadically.

There's a lot that isn't appreciated about outfielding. For openers, the real challenge is grounders, not flies. "We hit our outfielders 50 to 100 ground balls a day," said Lee Walls, who coached the A's. "Grounders are more important than flies." St. Louis, K.C., and San Diego utilityman Dane Iorg, experienced in infield and outfield alike, underscores another reason to take grounders. "If you field grounders, you keep your eye on the ball," he says. "That's all outfielding is—concentration."

Then there's the ongoing debate about catching with one or two hands. "The two-handed catch is a fallacy," says Snider. "Even when you catch two-handed, one hand is not really on the glove. The problem is assuming the big glove they use these days will catch the ball. You have to do it yourself."

Much attention is paid to how shallow outfielders play. Equal scrutiny should be given to the situations in which managers decide whether or not to bring their outfields in. With a man on third and no outs or one out in the ninth inning of a tie game, virtually any manager will bring in his outfield. The reason is simple: a routine or deep sacrifice fly will score the winning run. But what about this situation: man on *second*, tie score in the ninth? You'd think most managers would want to prevent a run-scoring single. Instead, they play their outfields at routine depth. "Well, they might hit one over our heads," managers invariably say. What they're really saying is, "I might be second-guessed." This practice is particularly egregious when left-fielders play deep for lefthanded batters and rightfielders for righthanders; few batters have power to the opposite field.

"It's easier to play outfield than infield," says Cincinnati player-manager Pete Rose, who has played everywhere and done everything. "The home run, RBI, and batting champions are usually outfielders. In the outfield there's less wear and tear warming up than in the infield and more time to concentrate on hitting. Outfielders don't lose weight over the course of a season, with the possible exception of centerfielders. You don't take a Dale Murphy or Dave Parker or Pedro Guerrero out of the lineup, unless they're hurt. But no matter where you play, you have to be aggressive. Even on AstroTurf. The only time you have to be really careful is when it's wet. The first time we played in Riverfront Stadium, it rained, and I think five outfielders made errors. The first bounce would be high, and the second would hug the ground. All the balls went under our gloves.

"Wherever you play, you have to go out there and practice taking balls off the fence. Players don't realize that the ball caroms differently off the Atlanta fence from the Cincinnati fence from the Shea fence from the Philadelphia fence. You need fungo batters to hit balls into the corners and off the fences. Another thing that players don't always know: any time a ball is hit within four feet of the foul line, you should concede a double and play the ball to prevent a triple. I've seen guys overrun the ball like they've never been out there. What it boils down to is doing your homework."

"The test of an outfielder's skill," Joe DiMaggio once said, "is when he has to go against a fence to make a catch." That was especially difficult when DiMaggio became a big leaguer because there were no warning tracks or padded fences. After the Dodgers' Pete Reiser suffered a concussion running into a concrete wall in 1947, the Dodgers installed a warning track and a padded fence. Other clubs soon followed suit.

Unfortunately, players have never learned to use the safety features properly. Still fearful of injury, they tend to turn their backs to the plate and cushion themselves with their arms as they hit the fence. When Willie Mays began coaching Giant outfielders in the spring of 1986, he set about correcting their lack of preparation.

"When you go into the fence, you use the fence to come back throwing," he told an audience consisting of Giant outfielders and Dave Anderson of *The New York Times*. "Don't let the fence use you. . . . The warning track is just what it says it is—a warning. . . . When the warning track lets you know you have time, you've got to turn."

Outfielder Jeffrey Leonard pretended to catch a fly, turned, backed into the fence, and let it propel him toward the infield.

"That's it," said Mays. "Now you are coming off the fence throwing."

"All these years nobody ever told me that before," said Leonard.

Finally, the overall worth of outfielding merits review. Granted, there's more action in the infield. The average outfielder handles two to three chances a game, the average third baseman three, shortstop four, second baseman five, and first baseman nine or ten. But there's another way of looking at the outfield. When an infielder makes a mistake, it usually costs one base. When an outfielder makes an error or misjudges a ball, it costs two, three, and sometimes four. Statistically, outfielding is tougher to judge than infielding. Some outfielders have gone entire seasons without committing errors but haven't been particularly useful. No range. On the other hand, speedy centerfielder Curt Flood handled a record 568 chances without error from September 3, 1965, to June 4, 1967. The best outfielding is more subtle than statistical: grabbing line drives hit in the alleys, holding shots down the lines to singles, taking away other hits with routine catches because of good positioning.

Who better to judge the worth of outfielders than the guy they help the most—the pitcher? "I owe my success," Lefty Gomez once said, "to clean living and a fast outfield."

LEWIS, SPEAKER, AND HOOPER

It was the golden age of outfielding, and they were the golden outfielders. In the first two decades of the twentieth century hitters swung cautiously and the ball stayed in the park. It wouldn't start shooting out until Babe Ruth and the lively ball got the homers rolling in the 1920s. There was no artificial turf to drive fielders back on their heels; that wouldn't be used until 1966. As a result, fielders played exceptionally shallow. So any ball hit over the infield was fair game for an outfielder's glove, and any baserunner was fair game for an outfielder's arm.

The glamour outfield of the glamour outfield era was the 1910–15 Boston threesome of Duffy Lewis in left, Tris (The Gray Eagle) Speaker in center, and Harry Hooper in right. They played equally well at two home parks—Huntington Avenue Grounds in 1910–11 and Fenway Park in 1912–15—and on the road. They were recruited by John I. Taylor, perhaps the only owner-scout in baseball history. And they could hit as well as field. In a letter to Red Sox' historian Ellery Clark, Hooper described how they came together:

"I played my first year, 1909, in left field. Started in right but couldn't handle the sun. . . . But while I played left . . . I practiced playing the sunfield until I was good at it. . . . In 1910

The outfield of the great Boston Red Sox clubs of the 1910s, left to right:
Duffy Lewis, Tris Speaker, Harry Hooper. *National Baseball Library*

Duffy Lewis came up. . . . But Duffy couldn't play the sunfield. So they shifted me to right and put Duffy in left. . . . That was the beginning of the outfield Lewis-Speaker-Hooper."

Speaker had started for Boston since 1909. In 1909–15 he led all American League centerfielders in total chances and put-outs per game five times and assists and double plays three times. Though all outfielders played more shallow than to-day's, Speaker popularized the idea of playing daringly close to the infield.[1] Indeed, he set a league record of four unassisted double plays by an outfielder.[2]

And that's not all he did. Speaker and Boston catcher "Rough" Bill Carrigan combined on a devilish play. As a baserunner set off to steal second, Speaker would rush in and Carrigan would deliberately throw the ball into center. The runner gleefully headed for third, only to be nailed there as Speaker took the "overthrow" on one hop and fired over.

Playing for the Red Sox from 1907 to 1915, the Indians from 1916 to 1926, the Senators in 1927, and the Athletics in 1928, Speaker set league outfield records of 6,791 putouts and 7,461 chances, and major league marks of 139 double plays and 448 assists. "Speaker . . . had that terrific instinct," Boston pitcher Smoky Joe Wood told Lawrence Ritter. "At the crack of the bat he'd be off with his back to the infield, and then he'd turn and glance over his shoulder at the last minute and catch the ball so easy it looked like there was nothing to it, nothing at all."

Many baseball experts (see centerfield section) rate Hall of Famer Speaker as the greatest centerfielder of all time. Hooper was surely the greatest rightfielder of the first half-century ("He was the closest I ever saw to Speaker as a fielder," Wood said). After moving to right from left, Hooper quickly built up his confidence and set an unofficial career rightfielder's record of 344 assists in his 17-year career (1909–20 with the Red Sox, 1921–25 with the White Sox), including 30 in 1910. Oh, yes. He also helped convince Boston manager Ed Barrow to make an everyday player of a pitcher named G. Herman Ruth.

Like Speaker, Hooper played with considerable flair. He invented the "rump slide," in which he made many a skidding catch of short flies. In the final game of the 1912 World Series,

1. Early centerfielders were situated shallower than leftfielders and rightfielders, who played away from the foul lines and probably fielded more balls in the gaps than they later would.

2. A minor league centerfielder named Walter Carlisle had the only unassisted triple play by an outfielder, in 1911.

with the Giants leading 1-0 in the sixth, Hooper ran down Larry Doyle's fly, leaped, hit the fence, spun around, caught the ball barehanded, and was in turn caught by the Boston fans as he fell into the stands. Boston went on to tie the game 1-1 in regulation and win it 3-2 in the tenth with the aid of two Giant fielding mistakes. Hooper was elected to the Hall of Fame despite a .281 lifetime batting average. He made it on his fielding, and he deserved it.

A knee injury cut short Duffy Lewis's Hall of Fame hopes and ended his career after 11 years (1910–17 with the Red Sox, 1919–20 with the Yankees, 1921 with the Senators). He batted .284 in both the regular season and three Series, and, like Hooper, is best remembered for his fielding. When the Red Sox moved from the Huntington Avenue Grounds to Fenway Park in 1912, Lewis was forced to play an 8- to 10-foot incline in deep left field. He mastered it so successfully it came to be known as "Duffy's Cliff."

"About 'Duffy's Cliff,'" Lewis wrote to Ellery Clark, "I used to go out and practice in the morning. You had to take one look at the ball. Go up if you had a chance to get it. You couldn't keep looking at the ball. If you did, down you went when you hit the bank."

Between 1910 and 1915 Hooper, Speaker, and Lewis joined forces in more than 90 percent of the Red Sox games. Did any outfield ever play together so regularly? Or so well?

11

Left Field: Left Out?

In the ultimate moment of a leftfielder's frustration, the Cubs' Dave Kingman uncorked a mighty throw that went ever so slightly off-line. The ball carried into the Chicago dugout, through the door, and into the adjoining bathroom, where it came to rest in a toilet bowl. "The immortal Dave 'Ding-Dong' Kingman," crowed *Chicago Tribune* columnist Mike Royko. "If he's ever voted into the Hall of Fame, they should put the toilet bowl there, too."

It's no accident that the expression "out of left field" connotes something ridiculous, farfetched, misplaced. As Kingman demonstrated, there's no end to the creativity leftfielders possess in mismanaging base hits, fly balls, and throws. The nastiest comment that can be made of an outfielder is, "He's got a leftfielder's arm." Not to mention a leftfielder's feet and judgment.

Perhaps the most aptly named player among this unfortunate breed is Lonnie (Skates) Smith, who slips and slides like a man on roller skates. Alas, there have been others too. Like Jay Johnstone, who once made the mistake of charging a sharply hit single on artificial turf; the ball caromed off his chest directly into the stands. And George (Showboat) Fisher, who hit .374 and fielded about as well in 1930; the next season he was back in the minors. And Smead Jolley (1930–33), who deserves a classification of his own.

As a White Sox player Jolley went into training for his left-field misadventures by mismanaging a more difficult position, right field. On a single play he let a hit bounce through his legs, carom off the fence, and bounce back through his legs. Whereupon he picked up the ball and heaved it over the third baseman's head. Obviously a man fit for left. He was traded to the Red Sox and promptly relocated in front of the Green Monster. In those days Fenway Park had an 8-to-10-foot incline instead of a warning track before the left-field wall. Red Sox coaches repeatedly hit fungoes to Jolley as he practiced running up the slope to make catches. Unfortunately, in a game against the Washington Senators he prematurely ran up the incline, only to discover the ball falling short. Jolley turned and started back down the incline but fell flat on his face, allowing the ball to drop and the runner to reach third. "Fine bunch, you guys," Jolley reportedly yelled at his coaches when he returned to the dugout. "For 10 days you teach me how to go up the hill, but none of you has the brains to teach me how to come down!"

Happily, there's more to our discussion of the leftfielder than ridicule. In fairness, it's not entirely his fault that the best defensive outfielders are located elsewhere; it's simply the nature of the three positions. Left field attracts the least talented players because it's the least challenging everyday position. A leftfielder never has to make the long throws centerfielders do, or attempt rightfielders' slingshots to third. A leftfielder who can run will be shifted to center as soon as he's needed there. Witness Willie Wilson, Tim Raines, and Rickey Henderson. A leftfielder who can throw probably started in right and will probably return there. Witness Dave Winfield. In short, leftfielders almost *have* to be slow and weak-armed.

"The centerfielder is the guy who can run," says Minnesota leftfielder Mickey Hatcher. "The rightfielder is the guy who can throw. The leftfielder is the guy who can hit." Indeed, if he's bad enough in the field, hitting is all some would-be leftfielders will do. It's no coincidence that among the best designated hitters have been some of the most hopeless or hobbled leftfielders: Greg Luzinski, Don Baylor, Kingman, and Mr. DH himself, Hal McRae. "My father told me, 'Son, you were born to hit,'" says designated hitter and occasional leftfielder Ron Kittle. "'If you want a Gold Glove, go buy one.'"

Not that there's no skill in playing left. In fact, the leftfielder faces a couple of challenges his outfield brethren don't. Let Winfield, who has considerable experience at all three outfield positions, explain. "When a runner is rounding third, a rightfielder or centerfielder can tell how far past the bag he is because the baseline is square to them," he says. "They can gauge their throws. Looking down the line, the leftfielder can't always tell how far the runner is from the bag. Also, because the runner is between him and home, the leftfielder is more likely to hit him on a scoring play than either of the other outfielders is." Leftfielder George Foster, then with Cincinnati, sent the unforgettable sixth game of the 1975 World Series into extra innings by throwing out Boston runner Denny Doyle at the plate. Foster's throw covered only 170 feet, but it was a considered a beauty because he sighted straight down the left-field line without hitting the runner.

In spite of his linear handicaps, the leftfielder probably throws out more runners at home than either the rightfielder or the centerfielder. The centerfielder invariably faces a long throw home and the rightfielder a relatively infrequent throw home. The leftfielder gets opportunities galore. He gets them not only because there are more righthanded batters pulling balls to left than lefthanders pulling to right, but because there are more lefthanded than righthanded batters hitting to the opposite field. Almost every lefty is taught to wait on the ball because he has a better chance to reach first by hitting to the left side of the infield than he does to the right. Further, a lefthander can poke a ball to left while he's running toward first; a righthander can't hit-and-run by himself without illegally crossing the plate. "We lefties are taught to hit to left because as kids we play in those shorthanded games where there's no hitting to right," adds former major league pitcher Jim Kaat. By contrast, a righty's right to pull is considered a birthright. The sight of a righthanded hitter riding a pitch to right is one of the most exquisite—and infrequent—in baseball.

Every time a runner reaches second, the leftfielder must gird himself to throw home on a base hit; with a runner on third and fewer than two outs, the leftfielder is thinking sacrifice fly. He must know what to do with either challenge: charge the ball as fast as possible, field it with his body set to throw, and let fly—all in the same fluid motion. "When you're throwing home, you aim for the cutoff man's chest," says KC's Willie Wilson. "That way, when he lets the ball go through, it reaches home on one bounce." When that happens, the fan gets one of the optimum moments of any game—a close play at the plate.

In addition to their 7-2 assists, leftfielders have made some memorable game-saving and otherwise spectacular catches. Maybe that's why the celebrated "Japanese catch" (see chapter one) was made in left. And maybe that's why some of the greatest World Series catches have been made by leftfielders: Al Gionfriddo in 1947, Sandy Amoros in 1955, Bob Allison in 1965, Joe Rudi in 1972, and a personal favorite, Lou Piniella in 1978.

In the sixth inning of the sixth game of the 1947 Series the Dodgers were protecting an 8-5 lead, when Dodger manager

UPI/Bettmann Newsphotos

Burt Shotton inserted an obscure outfielder named Al Gionfriddo as a defensive replacement in left. He came prepared for
the occasion, wearing a since-banned glove with a fishnet-like
"Red Rolfe web" featuring strips of rawhide from thumb to index finger. The Yankees put runners on first and second with
two outs, as George Stirnweiss walked and Yogi Berra singled
off lefthander Joe Hatten. Then Joe DiMaggio stepped up. We'll
let Red Barber call it from here:

"Swung on, belted. It's a long one, deep to left-center. Back
goes Gionfriddo. Back, back, back, back, back, back. He makes
a one-handed catch against the bullpen! Ohhhhh, *doctor*!"

Oakland's Joe Rudi's game-saving catch of Denis Menke's drive in the second game of the 1972 World Series against Cincinnati, left; and, above, the
longtime New York Yankees outfielder, and most recently manager, Lou
Piniella. *New York Yankees*

DiMaggio had swung at Hatten's first pitch and sent it toward the left-field fence. Gionfriddo had run back desperately,
turning this way and that like an escaping burglar, and leaped
at the last minute to catch the ball at the 415-foot mark. In
a rare display of public disgust DiMaggio, who was about to
round second by the time the ball was caught, kicked the dirt
in front of him. As the Dodgers hung on to win 8-6 and post-

Brooklyn's Sandy Amoros has just made his running catch of Yogi Berra's fly ball in the sixth inning of the final game of the 1955 World Series, and is turning to fire to Pee Wee Reese, who will relay the ball to Gil Hodges to double up Gil McDougald. The Dodgers whipped the Yankees 2–0 to take their first World Series ever. The umpire is John Flaherty.
UPI/Bettmann Newsphotos

pone their Series loss until the next day, the catch immediately became immortalized: an obscure player robbing an immortal, the underdogs holding off the perennial champs.

In 1955, with a major assist from Amoros, the Dodgers won their first Series title. Johnny Podres clinched the finale of the seven-game Series by shutting out the Yankees 2-0; without Amoros, the score would have been tied 2-2 with a Yankee on third and no one out in the sixth. That inning Junior Gilliam had been shifted from left to second and Amoros inserted in left. New York's Billy Martin walked to open the inning, and Gil McDougald reached base with a bunt single. With men on first and second and the lefthanded-hitting Yogi Berra up, Amoros shaded toward center. He appeared to have made the wrong move when Berra sliced a fly ball barely inside the left-field foul line. With Martin and McDougald moving, Amoros raced toward the line, grabbed the ball, and braced himself on the low wire outfield fence. Righting himself, Amoros threw to shortstop Pee Wee Reese, who relayed to first baseman Gil Hodges to double up McDougald.

Minnesota's Allison caught Jim Lefebvre's sinking liner and skidded 20 feet across the left-field line, setting up the Twins' 3-1 win over LA in Game Two of the 1965 Series. As Oakland beat Cincinnati 2-1 in the second game of the 1972 Series, the A's Rudi supplied both the big home run and the big defensive play. With a runner on first and one out in the top of the ninth, the Reds' Denis Menke hit a line drive toward the left-field wall. Rudi leaped up four feet as he was turning to his right and caught the drive; photos of the play suggested he was clinging to the fence like a human fly. Had the catch not been made, Hal McRae's following single would have scored one and possibly two runs.

A number of leftfielders' catches—by the Philadelphia Athletics' Rube Oldring in the 1913 Series and by the Red Sox' Duffy Lewis in the 1915 Series—weren't pivotal enough to be included in *World Series Records* writeups. Nor was Piniella's play in 1978, but it unquestionably deserves to be played and replayed before drama classes. Piniella went over the fence in Yankee Stadium and came down with his glove closed against his body. For several seconds he walked back toward his position. No one knew if he'd caught the ball or not. Then he pulled it out of his glove and threw it to the infield. Take a bow, Lou.

What is it about the Yankees? Babe Ruth closed out the 1928 World Series by racing across the left-field foul line amid showering paper and scorecards to make a one-handed catch of a foul pop hit by Frankie Frisch. Ruth held the ball aloft, never broke stride, and continued into the Yankee clubhouse. In 1965 Tom Tresh preserved a tie game in the tenth by vaulting several rows into the stands to rob the White Sox' Danny Cater (Tresh subsequently won the game by homering in the Yankees' tenth). "Right up there with the very best I've ever seen," said Yankee manager Johnny Keane. "I never saw an outfielder jump so far into the stands to make a catch." In 1981 Winfield literally climbed the padded left-field fence—sticking a cleat into it, in fact—to rob Baltimore's Doug DeCinces of a sure homer. Eyewitnesses who hadn't been to Japan called it the greatest defensive play in history. In 1985 another New York leftfielder, Ken Griffey, made plays resembling the Amoros and Winfield catches.

Yes, there are good leftfielders. Some of them, such as Lewis and the Dodgers' Andy Pafko, were playing in outfields so strong there was no room for them in right or center. But there are others who elected, for one reason or another, to make a go of it at baseball's least noted position: Rudi, Chick Hafey, Jose Cruz, Zack Wheat, and Carl Yastrzemski (see profile).

It seems worthwhile, therefore, to hear the encomium former Houston manager Bob Lillis delivered on behalf of his left-fielder Jose Cruz a few years ago. "Jose worked very hard to become a good fielder. He ranks near the top in effort and enthusiasm. He gets such a good jump on the ball he's able to make those leaps against the fence and diving catches on short flies. He's terrific at going to the line and holding runners to singles. And he comes in on the ball well and uses his great arm strength and accuracy to make throws to the plate."

Like any honest workman striving to master his trade, Cruz put in many hours of hard work. Any accomplished leftfielder has done the same. Yet it's the nature of left—or the position's reputation—that critics have the last laugh. "Gionfriddo?" they scoff. "He turned the wrong way before making the catch and never played in another big-league game. Amoros? He flat disappeared. They can't even locate him for old-timers' games!"

So pity the poor leftfielder. In the universe of baseball defense, he's a dull, distant star: left out.

CARL YASTRZEMSKI

The Red Sox were leading the A's by three runs in the eighth inning of their third 1975 playoff game when Oakland's Reggie Jackson hit a hard shot to left-center that threatened to leave two runners in scoring position. The ball bounced twice and then, suddenly and unexpectedly, Boston leftfielder Carl Yastrzemski hauled it down with a desperation dive. Outfielders routinely dive for line drives and long flies and Texas leaguers, but rarely for balls that have already bounced. But Yastrzemski dived, caught it, held Jackson to a single, and ultimately saved the game. It was the ultimate play by the ultimate left-fielder.

Yastrzemski will make the Hall of Fame as a hitter, but he deserves enshrinement for his glove as well. Although he fin-

The Red Sox' Carl Yastrzemski, master of the "Green Monster" in left field at Fenway Park in Boston, is shown here taking third base on Amos Otis's fly ball in the 1970 All-Star Game. Bill Grabarkewitz of the Los Angeles Dodgers is taking the ball. *UPI/Bettmann Newsphotos*

ished his career as a first baseman and designated hitter, he played more games (3,308) than anyone in American League history and surely logged more time in left than anyone too. The results, though less noted than his hitting, were equally impressive.

Reporting to the Red Sox in 1961, Yaz immediately faced two challenges any leftfielder would have dreaded. First, he was succeeding Ted Williams, who had just retired. Williams wore number nine on his uniform; Yastrzemski was pointedly given number eight. And if it wasn't enough to replace an immortal in left, Yaz immediately came face-to-face with the Green Monster, the 37-foot-high left-field wall in Fenway Park that takes a minute to love and a lifetime to learn.

Yastrzemski did both. In the beginning he suffered numerous embarrassments from balls caroming past him off the wall and out of the difficult left-field corner. By 1967, the year he won the Triple Crown and led the Red Sox to their Impossible Dream pennant, he came to know the Monster not only by sight but by sound. The bottom 15 feet at the time were made of cement. "When you heard it hit the cement wall, you stayed back a ways because it came off hard," Yastrzemski told *Sports Illustrated's* Bill Nack. "Above the cement, you had squares of tin with rivets in them. If the ball hit the tin, it made a thud, and the ball dropped straight down. If it hit the rivets, it could do anything, come straight down, shoot to the side."

Yastrzemski likes to talk of his "tough Polish stock" and his love of privacy, and he made himself a great leftfielder by hard and lonely practice. He had one advantage, however, over most of his peers. Yaz had been signed as a shortstop, and he charged base hits with the confidence of a natural infielder. "You don't run on his arm," became an axiomatic expression around the American League. Nonetheless, Yastrzemski led all AL outfielders in assists seven times and won seven Gold Gloves.

Early in 1967 teammate Billy Rohr had a no-hitter going in Yankee Stadium when Tom Tresh hit a shot toward the left-field fence. "Everyone thought, 'That's it—the no-no's over,'" Red Sox infielder Dalton Jones told the *Boston Globe's* Bob Duffy years later. "Carl turned his back on the ball—just flat-out turned his back on it—and started running and running for the fence. When he got to the fence, he turned and dove and caught the ball. We all looked at each other and said, 'Man, that's just not supposed to happen.'"

That play, Jones feels, set the tone for Yastrzemski's entire 1967 season. By the last five weeks he was carrying the team with both his bat and glove. Fittingly, in the final game of the season he went 4-for-4 at the plate and made the game's key fielding play when he surprisingly threw behind the lead runner and caught Minnesota's Bob Allison straining for a double.

His great batting and fielding moments often went together. In the 1967 Series he hit .400 and made all the plays in left. In the 1975 Series Yaz batted .310 and made an extraordinary diving catch. But that was nothing compared to perhaps his greatest demonstration of all-around play ever, in the preceding three-game playoff series against Oakland. Though he'd played only eight games in left all season, Yaz fielded superbly. He threw out Bert Campaneris and Sal Bando at third in the second game and Reggie Jackson twice at second in the clincher, and in the final coup de grace held Jackson to that eighth-inning single. In the series Yastrzemski also batted .455. No matter. "The thing I remember most," he said afterward, "is defense."

12

Center Field:
A Dream Come True

So I ran all right, out of the hospital and up to the playground and right out to center field, the position I play for a softball team that wears silky blue-and-gold jackets with the name of the club scrawled in big white felt letters from one shoulder to the other: SEABEES, A.C. Thank God for the Seabees, A.C.! Thank God for center field! Doctor, you can't imagine how truly glorious it is out there, so alone in all that space. . . . Do you know baseball at all? Because center field is like some observation post, a kind of control tower, where you are able to see everything and everyone, to understand what's happening the instant it happens, not only by the sound of the struck bat, but by the spark of movement that goes through the infielders in the first second that the ball comes flying at them; and once it gets beyond them, "It's mine," you call, "it's mine," and then after it you go. For in center field, if you can get to it, it *is* yours. Oh, how unlike my home it is to be in center field, where no one will appropriate unto himself anything that I say is *mine*!

—PHILIP ROTH, *Portnoy's Complaint*

Center field is a boy's dream come true. "You can see the ball off the bat, you can run for it and you're in charge of the whole outfield," says former utilityman Bob Bailor, who played full-time for two seasons in Toronto. "You can run as far as you want and throw as far as you want—as long as you hit the cutoff man. It's like you're a kid in your backyard again."

The prototypical centerfielder is a consummation of that childhood dream: a rangy soldier constantly making over-the-shoulder catches and hitting game-winning homers. He can do it all—hit, run, throw, and field. He has powerful arms sticking out from under that jersey—no wimpy sweatshirt to protect him. He takes a full cut and follows through with both hands on the bat, unlike the many moderns who let go with one hand like some tennis player. And, of course, he's the very model of comportment.

If the name Dale Murphy comes blasting to mind, it should. Through the mid-1980s the Atlanta star had become one of baseball's best all-around players, and certainly its best all-around centerfielder. When he fouls a line drive into the stands,

"TRIS" SPEAKER, Center Fielder
BOSTON RED SOX
WORLD CHAMPIONS 1915

Tris Speaker, the "Gray Ghost," above; and Dale
Murphy, Atlanta Braves, right. *National Baseball Library*

he looks anxiously after it, concerned that he may have injured
someone. He's almost too good to be true. He's a centerfielder.

In baseball's best-played era, 1947–60,[1] the most noted players were centerfielders—Willie Mays, Mickey Mantle, Duke
Snider, Joe DiMaggio. Talk about lyrical legends: one of the
first great centerfielders was a man named Fielder Jones. Of all
the heroes Simon and Garfunkel could have cited in their 1968
hit song, "Mrs. Robinson," they chose Joe DiMaggio ("Where

1. The span between the integration of baseball and the modern era's first major
expansion.

Atlanta Journal-Constitution

have you gone, Joe DiMaggio? / A nation turns its lonely eyes to you"). In "Talkin' Baseball," the popular album Terry Cashman cut in 1982, he leads off with a song called, "Willie, Mickey and 'The Duke.'" And in 1985 John Fogerty sings to his coach of his highest ambition: "Look at me / I can be / Center field."

Why is center so centralized in baseball tradition? Sure, there's the feeling of owning the world when you're camped out there in the middle of the outfield. There's also the way the position has been best played. A centerfielder would run off the end of the earth to catch a ball. From Tris Speaker to Cool

Joe DiMaggio, Yankees, above; and Mickey Mantle, Yankees, right.
New York Yankees

Papa Bell to Paul Blair, the best of them played so shallow they were almost fifth infielders. They'd dare the batter to hit one over them and then run it down, catch it, and maybe for good measure make some prodigious throw to hold the runner. In all, there's a gunslinger's bravado about the shallow-situated, strong-armed centerfielder. Go ahead, he seems to be telling the batter, make my day.

"And I could field, too," said Portnoy, "and the farther I had to run, the better. 'I got it! I got it! I got it!' and tear in toward second, to trap in the webbing of my glove—and barely an inch off the ground—a

New York Yankees

ball driven hard and low and right down the middle, a base hit, someone thought . . . Or back I go, 'I got it, I got it'—back easily and grace-
fully toward that wire fence, moving practically in slow motion, and
then that delicious DiMaggio sensation of grabbing it like something
heaven-sent over one shoulder . . . Or running! turning! leaping! . . .
Or just standing nice and calm—nothing trembling, everything se-
rene—standing there in the sunshine (as though in the middle of an
empty field, or passing the time on the street corner), standing without a care in the world in the sunshine, like my king of kings, the Lord
my God, The Duke Himself (Snider, Doctor, the name may come up
again), standing there as loose and as easy, as happy as I will ever be,
just waiting by myself under a high fly ball. . . ."

Alas, center field has changed some since the days of Willie, Mickey, The Duke, and DiMag, not to mention Portnoy's fantasies. For one thing, artificial turf came along in the 1960s. It drove the peerless warrior away from the infield, made him a shade cautious; fearful of whippet shots that would skip off the carpet in left-center and right-center and carry to the wall, he was forced to play deeper and cut off balls that were already hits rather than catch those that might be. As a result, the very nature of the centerfielder's position is different. Now the accent isn't on his arm as much as his speed. Sure, there are strong-armed, power-hitting centerfielders like Murphy, but there seem to be more roadrunners: Gary Pettis, Willie Wilson, Brett Butler, John Cangelosi, Willie McGee, Bob Dernier, Rickey Henderson, Mookie Wilson.

With the revisionist modern centerfielder, there's also a revisionist argument about the worth of the position. "Center's easier than the other outfield positions," says Snider. "You see the ball come off the bat better and it doesn't hook or slice as much as it does to left or right. Also, you have room to roam, and you don't have to contend with walls as much."

There's some truth to this. A leftfielder's view of a batted ball may be partially blocked by a righthanded hitter, a rightfielder's view by a lefthander; they won't pick up the ball as quickly as a centerfielder, who can more clearly see the ball and batter. "You can see if the pitch is going to be inside or outside," says centerfielder Tony Armas, the former A's rightfielder. And, yes, the ball does move in strange parabolas toward the foul lines, as opposed to the relatively straightahead path it takes toward center. But those straight shots aren't perfectly straight. "Sometimes they'll jump around like a knuckleball or take off on you," says Pete Rose. "When a lefthanded batter hits a ball toward your left shoulder, it'll wind up over your right shoulder because of a slight slice," says Toronto rightfielder Jesse Barfield, who occasionally fills in at center. "If a righthander hits it toward your right shoulder, it'll wind up over your left. I think it's easier to switch from center to right than from right to center."

The centerfielder has far greater responsibilities than his outfield mates. For openers, he must catch the ball more often—up to 25 percent more often. In the 1970s, to take a typical decade, no non-centerfielder ever led the majors in putouts. The centerfielder has more ground to cover than the others and, being the fastest outfielder, is expected to catch anything he can reach.

Bobby Murcer of the New York Yankees. *New York Yankees*

Indeed, the quickest of today's breed, California's Gary Pettis, covers fully 35,000 square feet in Anaheim Stadium, or so head groundskeeper Brian Nofziger told *Sports Illustrated*'s Bruce Anderson. If the centerfielder takes primary responsibility for balls in the gap, the rightfielder and leftfielder can shade toward the lines to play those curving and caroming shots to the corners. Maybe the centerfielder doesn't play as many wall shots, but he does play them. And the centerfielder has to back up his mates on balls hit to them and decide who's to catch balls hit between himself and another fielder. "I am," Henderson says grandly, "the captain of the outfield."

Yet he still has to edge in toward second base every chance he gets. Bobby Murcer, the old Yankee centerfielder, explains why. "You play shallow because, as a rule, more balls will be hit in front of you than behind you. It's also important to play shallow because, in spite of what you might think, it's harder to catch a ball coming in than going back. When you're running in, you're often trying to catch the ball by reaching down to your knees or lower. That's tougher than catching it at eye level, which is the way you normally do and the way you do when you're running back."

"You've got to know the hitters," says Andre Dawson, a long-time centerfield stalwart who switched to right when his knees started to go. "You think about who's capable of hitting the ball over your head, what the situation is, who's pitching, and how good his stuff is. I like to play shallow because I feel I can go back on the ball as well as I can come in. It's a challenge when the ball's hit deep. What I do is run to the spot where I think the ball's going to come down and then turn around. Late in the ball game, when you're up a few runs, you can afford to play a little deeper. But when you play shallow, you have the chance to take away line drives. It depends on how much confidence you have in yourself."

"The field dictates how deep you play," says Baltimore's Fred Lynn. "In Boston the grass is high, so you can move up. In California the ball scoots through, so you have to play deeper." A good thing Lynn did, or he wouldn't have made an unforgettable catch when he was with California on September 21, 1982. KC's Amos Otis had hit a deep drive to left-center, and Lynn and leftfielder Brian Downing converged on it at the wall. As they barely avoided a collision, Downing ran into the padded fence, shoving it back and allowing Lynn to reach over and make a sensational catch. But Lynn has happier memories still. "What I really like," he says, "is playing on a wet field. That way I'm almost certain to make a sliding catch."

As any outfielder will tell you, the toughest balls to field are those hit right at him. For an instant—often a fatal instant—he can't tell if the ball will drop in front of him or carry over his head. Failing to come in on time yields only a single, but imagine the embarrassment of the fielder who starts in, only to reverse himself a second too late. Many is the converted left-fielder or rightfielder turned into a corkscrew by a ball hit over his head. "When you're going back," says Snider, "you have to turn the right way and know which way the ball is going to be pushed by the wind. That's why we take fielding practice."

Oh, the endless variety of great moments in center! Willie Mays's catch off Vic Wertz in the 1954 World Series was possibly the most famous play ever by a major league outfielder. It wasn't, however, the greatest catch ever made by a centerfielder or a centerfielder named Mays (see profile). The best catch Duke Snider remembers making seems at least comparable. "I was going after a drive hit by Puddin' Head Jones one afternoon in Philadelphia," he says. "I went about 10 feet up the wall and caught my spikes in a groove. But I caught the ball and hung onto it when I went crashing down." He smiles. "And the game was on the line at the time."

There was the sliding, barehanded catch the Cardinals' Terry Moore made off the Giants' Mel Ott during the 1936 season; Moore also slid into the wall to avoid a collision and catch a drive by another Giant, Morrie Arnovich, in 1941. Old-timers remember those catches even though they didn't occur during critical late-season games or the Series. The same could be said of Joe DiMaggio's catch off Detroit's Hank Greenberg in 1939; back to the plate, the Yankee Clipper ran to the Miller Huggins monument 461 feet out, instinctively reached up and grabbed the ball as it disappeared in the shadows. (Eloquently responding, the Tigers rose in the dugout, salaamed, and doffed their caps.) A lifelong fan named Bruce Erricson writes of a catch he saw the Cardinals' Curt Flood make in Candlestick Park. "I was seated in the front row of the right-centerfield bleachers when someone hit a bullet to the fence, a sure double or triple. Out of nowhere Flood outran the ball, catching it over his head, glove outstretched, at full-speed, two steps in front of the wire-mesh fence they had at the time. Then, instead of bracing himself to crash into the fence, he somehow managed to put his leg up, carom off the fence, and throw back to the infield, all in one motion. I still don't know how he did it without breaking his ankle."

There's a purity of line to most celebrated catches by centerfielders. They all seem to involve endless runs or magnificent leaps, or at the very least come at timely moments. On June 3, 1932, Aloysius Harry (Al) Simmons of the Philadelphia Athletics ran into deep left-center, leaped, and one-handed a drive by the Yankees' Lou Gehrig. If Simmons had missed the ball, it would have bounded into the corner behind the bleachers and possibly given Gehrig a record fifth homer in one game. On April 30, 1946, Hall of Fame pitcher Bob Lemon, then playing center, ran more than 100 feet to catch DiMaggio's wind-blown fly and save Bob Feller's no-hitter.

In 1975 Lynn, then playing for the Red Sox, made a catch that just about knocked the Yankees out of the American League's East Division race. He dived, bounced three times, and lay sprawled on the warning track after one-handing a ninth-inning drive to preserve a 1-0 win. In the 1936 Series the Giants' Hank Leiber robbed DiMaggio on a 460-foot shot in the deepest part of the Polo Grounds. And in the 1942 Series Moore went clear to the Yankee Stadium monuments to take an extra-base blow away from poor DiMag. No one seems to have been robbed by more circus catches than Jolted Joe, the Yankee Clipped.

All those epic runs and sterling grabs take their toll. A right-fielder or leftfielder switches to center when he's young and speedy. A centerfielder switches to right or left when his legs start to go. "Center's a great position to play," says Bobby Murcer, "as long as you're about 22." For all its changes, center field remains the position for youth and dreams and legend. As it was to Portnoy:

"And it's true, is it not?—incredible, but apparently true—there are people who feel in life the ease, the self-assurance, the simple and essential affiliation with what is going on, that I used to feel as the center fielder for the Seabees? Because it wasn't, you see, that one was the best center fielder imaginable, only that one knew exactly, and down to the smallest particular, how a center fielder should conduct himself. And there are people like that walking the streets of the U.S. of A.? I ask you, why can't I be one! Why can't I exist now as I existed for the Seabees out there in center field! Oh, to be a center fielder, a center fielder—and nothing more!"

WILLIE MAYS

"I believed that when I went on that field that I was on stage."—Willie Mays

Willie Mays was not a purist's centerfielder. He once committed four errors in a single game; Joe DiMaggio stopped the earth on the rare days he made one. Mays didn't reach everything and sometimes threw parabolas to his cutoff men; Richie Ashburn, for one, covered more ground. Mays never led the National League in fielding percentage, and only led once each in putouts and assists; Tris Speaker led the American League twice in fielding, seven times in putouts, and three times in assists. And Mays never had a Series like Cincinnati's Edd Roush, who made nine great catches in 1919. In 1972 the Society for American Baseball Research (SABR) polled the fielding experts among its membership to determine the greatest outfielder of all time. Each voter was asked to name the three best, regardless of position. Speaker finished first with 19 of a possible 24

Perhaps the finest centerfielder of all time, Willie Mays of the
Giants. *San Francisco Giants*

votes, followed by Mays, with 15. Since both Speaker and Mays
were centerfielders, the vote could have established Speaker as
the position's greatest ever.

But not to Hall of Fame rightfielder Harry Hooper, who
played beside Speaker on the 1909–15 Red Sox. "That Willie
Mays," Hooper told Lawrence S. Ritter in *The Glory of Their
Times*, "he's one of the greatest centerfielders who ever lived.
You can go back as far as you want and name all the great
ones—Tris Speaker, Eddie Roush, Max Carey, Earle Combs, Joe
DiMaggio. I don't care *who* you name, Mays is just as good,
maybe better. He's a throwback to the old days, a guy who can
do everything, and plays like he loves it."

Center field is above all a theatrical position, and Mays was
the greatest actor ever to play it. It's the position that requires a
man to make not only the routine plays, but the spectacular.
Statistics don't fully describe the position; stage presence does.
"Fans hate to see a dull game," Mays says. "I always tried to
make it interesting. I was an entertainer."

In his starring role Mays consistently led the league in running out from under his cap and in making barehanded catches; he also, of course, popularized the basket catch. Mays could decoy runners into thinking he'd lost a ball, only to magically recover and throw them out. He was always where the action and excitement were: he led league outfielders four times in double plays and had more chances (7,431) than any outfielder in baseball history.

By the age of 16 Mays was starting for the Birmingham Black Barons, a team in the old Negro Leagues, and playing brilliant if orthodox center field. Indeed, according to *New York Post* columnist Maury Allen, Mays didn't begin making the basket catch in pro ball until his second full year in the majors. He had been Rookie of the Year in 1951. After 34 games the following season, Mays was drafted into the military. He began experimenting with his fielding, picked up the basket catch, and discovered he could catch well with it and throw better. "When he returned to the Giants in 1954, the Dodgers had been drawing better than the Giants and Mays's manager, Leo Durocher, urged him to come up with something new," says Allen. "He said, 'Do anything you want, as long as you catch the ball.' That's when Willie began using the basket catch full-time."

Arguing about Mays's greatest play, people quickly dismiss the catch on Vic Wertz in the eighth inning of the 1954 Series opener. Granted, Mays did run to a point 450 feet from home with his back to the plate to catch the ball; yes, he did uncork a splendid throw to keep Larry Doby from scoring after he'd tagged up and advanced from second to third; true, Mays prevented the Indians from breaking open a 2-2 game, and the Giants won 5-2 in the tenth. No matter. Mays claims he made a better play in the top of the tenth when he backhanded a Wertz liner bounding into left-center, holding him to a double instead of an inside-the-park homer.

And there were others that should rank ahead of the Wertz catch. In 1952 Mays made a headfirst dive to grab a shot by Bobby Morgan, slammed into the wall, and fell unconscious. "The next thing I know," Mays said later, "Leo Durocher was bending over me and asking if I was all right." Jackie Robinson told Mays it was the greatest catch he'd ever seen.

Ah, but Mays did better still. "I remember once at Candlestick," he told Ron Fimrite of *Sports Illustrated*, "Bobby Bonds and I went up for a ball in right center. Bobby never did learn how to climb a fence, so I went up and caught it. When I came down, I hit his knee. It knocked me out, but I held onto the ball." And saved a 2-1 Giant win.

Like all great centerfielders, Mays played shallow. So shallow that broadcaster Bill White, the old Cardinal and Phillie first baseman, swears he saw him catch a ball in the *infield*. "The second baseman misjudged the ball, and Willie caught it between first and second," White says.

It's somehow possible to imagine Mays making these catches. His occasional barehanded catches almost defy credibility. "Frank Thomas had huge hands and took pride in being able to catch balls barehanded that guys threw as hard as they could from the pitcher's mound," says Allen. "One day Mays took up the challenge and caught Thomas's fastball barehanded. Willie just had these amazing hands that could give with the ball."

"Don't call them hard hands," says Mays. "If your hands are hard, the ball drops out. If they're soft, the ball stays in."

Duke Snider saw Mays dive and barehand a ball on the warning track in the Polo Grounds. Hal Lanier, a former teammate of Mays, saw him run for a liner in left-center, reach out with his glove, and then reach past his glove to barehand it. And there was another barehand catch, one that Mays made 450 feet from the plate to rob Roberto Clemente in Forbes Field. Branch Rickey, who was general manager of the Pirates at the time, called *that* the greatest catch he ever saw. Bill Guifoile, publicity director at the Hall of Fame, has asked fans, writers, and ex-players to send him their favorite fielding plays. The player most often mentioned in their letters is Willie Howard Mays.

But how does one isolate moments in the theater of center? Describing Willie Mays's greatest fielding play is about as easy as spotlighting Sir Laurence Olivier's greatest moment on stage. Willie was just one continuous showstopper. Say, hey!

13

Right Field: The Best Is Last

"Hey, the kid's bad news. Let's play eight on a side—no hittin' to right."
—From the opening scene of the musical revue, "Diamonds."

Regard the rightfielder. Misunderstood and underrated, he's one of baseball's most enigmatic figures. In the sandlots he's either left out or last chosen. He's the little kid exiled from second base, the fat boy expelled from catcher, the not-quite-fast-enough centerfielder. At higher levels the rightfielder remains a disgruntled refugee from another position. Not until he reaches the majors does he attain his singular stature: master of corner and wall, conqueror of sunlight and twilight, long bowman with the on-target arm. But at every level the rightfielder remains number nine on our scorecards and last in our hearts.

Every so often baseball perks up and takes notice of the position. Such a year was 1984, when the Padres' Tony Gwynn led the majors in hitting, the Cubs' Keith Moreland and the Tigers' Kirk Gibson made critical playoff catches, and Gibson contributed a key throw and two decisive homers in the Series. The major leagues were loaded with quality rightfielders. And the hottest new player anywhere was a rightfielder. Guy named Hobbs. Roy Hobbs. They called him *The Natural.*

As it happens, naturals have long abounded in right field. There are 20 rightfielders in the Hall of Fame—more than any other position but pitcher. Among these immortals are Hank Aaron, Babe Ruth, Mel Ott, Paul Waner, Frank Robinson, Al Kaline, and the peerless gloveman, Roberto Clemente (see profile).

How could the weakest everyday position in amateur ball become the strongest in major league history? "In organized ball you're always going to have good hitters in right," says Kaline. "Up-the-middle players—catchers, second, short, and center—concentrate on their fielding. The other players—first, third, left, and right—can concentrate more on their hitting." The rightfielder makes baseball's longest throw—as long as 450 feet for anyone who could heave the ball from deepest right to

The Detroit Tigers' Al Kaline. *Detroit Tigers*

third base in the old Polo Grounds. It makes sense that the guy with the strongest arm should also hit for most power.

To fans, the greatest feat by an outfielder is surely his most spectacular catch. Outfielders view themselves differently. "I think my best plays have just been good throws," says Boston rightfielder Dwight Evans. "Making a good throw gives me the same feeling as hitting a homer." By and large, throws are more challenging than catches. As former Yankee outfielder Tommy Henrich used to say, "Catching a fly ball is a pleasure, but knowing what to do with it after you catch it is a business."

No one has known what to do with a ball like the rightfielder. Indeed, there's a surreal quality to their throws. From the Cardinals' Enos Slaughter cutting down the Yankees' Tuck Stainback in the 1942 Series to latter-day Card George Hendrick nabbing Milwaukee's Robin Yount in 1982 to any of a thousand pegs by Clemente, rightfielders have made throws to third that had the tautness of 300-foot clotheslines strung across the sky.

Only a rightfielder could throw out a batter at first—9-3 if you're scoring—on would-be singles. That was an accident of his positioning. But only the rightfielder seems to perform miracles his outfield brethren are no less capable of. With the bases loaded, the Yankees' Cliff Mapes caught a line drive on one bounce and made a throw home that forced the Red Sox' Johnny Pesky coming in from third. The Dodgers' Carl Furillo was so feared that when he caught a one-bouncer, the runner on third wouldn't always *try* to score. "Nobody ever goes from first to third on Dwight Evans," former American Leaguer Enos Cabell once said. "Never has, never will." Not until Boston's Evans began acting human in his mid-thirties.

Well, the rightfielder had better know how to throw. "He has to keep runners from advancing more than any other position," says former Baltimore rightfielder Ken Singleton. "Sometimes, when a single is hit to center, the runner can't go from first to third." When the ball is hit down the line, righthanded rightfielders must make 360-degree turns while throwing. What's more, all rightfielders routinely field grounders on the run if they hope to get runners on third. "You have to charge the ball, slow up a little before you get to it, and try to get a good hop," says Evans, who has been making the play at Fenway Park since 1972. "Then make a curve around the ball so that you're lined up in the direction you want to throw."

There's no outfield scene as tense as the sight of a rightfielder charging a single while a baserunner rounds second. If the throw to third is late, there may be runners on second and third. If the rightfielder makes enough good throws, the runners hold up and no throw is necessary. It's the difference between two runners in scoring position and two runners in double play position.

The best fielders cherish the challenge. Hence, the profile of the optimum rightfielder: aggressive, confident, even cocky. "I've watched tapes of Clemente," says the Cardinals' Andy Van Slyke, one of the National League's best defensive rightfielders. "He loved it when a guy challenged him. I try to be like that. You'll never hear a coach yell at an outfielder for being too aggressive. I always charge the ball. Sometimes I'll bobble it and the runner will wind up at second or third or home. If I hadn't been aggressive, he'd be there anyway. There's nothing like the outfielder who tells the runner, 'I dare you to run.'"

Sometimes he'll do so with relish. When the Yankees' Rickey Henderson reaches first against Toronto, he'll look out to rightfielder Jesse Barfield and wiggle his legs. Barfield, who led all

AL outfielders with 20 assists in 1986, responds by blowing on his index finger like a gunslinger clearing the smoke from his six-gun. "Some runners will tell me to back up and give them a chance. I tell them 'No way—don't even try.'" If they're foolish enough to go for extra bases, Barfield is prepared. Before games he and shortstop Tony Fernandez play "long toss," a 200-foot game of catch that stretches out their arms. Barfield also plays a baseball-style "21" with centerfielder Lloyd Moseby. "If he catches my throw at his belt buckle I get one point," says Barfield. "Two for the chest, three for the head. You get in the habit of hitting the target."

The challenging throw isn't all that confronts a newcomer to right. Tricky to learn and tough to play, the position demands an especially resilient athlete. It's accepted that line drives and fly balls come relatively straight at centerfielders but hook or slice at rightfielders and leftfielders; well, the English on the ball is considerably weirder for a rightfielder than a leftfielder. Most balls hit to leftfielders are thrown by righthanders and batted by righthanders. When the pitcher throws the ball, it's likely to come at a batter with a left-to-right motion; the batter hits it with a right-to-left motion. The ball may still move crazily off his bat, but the countervailing motions are likely to straighten it out a bit. Balls hit to right are usually thrown by righthanders and hit by lefthanders: two left-to-right motions producing wicked hooks. "The ball comes at you like a banana," says former Detroit rightfielder Pat Sheridan.

But not always. "The ball doesn't curve toward the line every time because some righthanded hitters can drive it up the gap," says Keith Moreland. Says Evans, "Three batters used to give me fits. Tony Oliva's hits would hook or sink or rise over my head—he made me feel like a fool. Cecil Cooper hits balls that take off to my right; you don't see that from other lefthanded hitters. Graig Nettles would hit balls with topspin and bite. You think it'll be easy, and you wind up diving."

No wonder rightfielders work harder than anyone at getting a good jump on the ball. "My speed was not a big factor in my fielding—my jump was," says Rusty Staub, who played right for much of his 23-year career. "When I came up to the Astros, a coach, Jim Busby, taught us outfielders how to get a jump. He'd hit us line drive after line drive from about 150 feet away. Eventually we'd learn how to see the ball off the bat. Then Busby would lengthen out his hits. I also did everything I could to know the pitchers and hitters. I'd talk to the catcher about how he'd call the game, and during the game get the signals from the catcher, shortstop, or second baseman."

A good rightfielder should back up first on any throw that could go down the line. Nonetheless, a rightfielder's worst enemy may be sheer boredom. Since he touches the ball less often than any player, he constantly fights the urge to daydream. "I expect the ball to be hit to me 27 times a game," says Van Slyke. "That's how I keep my head in the game. I keep asking questions: 'If the ball's hit down the line, is Keith Hernandez or Mookie Wilson running?' I keep going over situations that might happen. That way I won't be surprised."

Oddly, the easiest transition to right may be that from the most dissimilar position on the field: catcher. Says Moreland, who moved from behind the plate to the outfield in 1983, "It helped that I'd played in a position where I had to concentrate all the time. It also helped that a coach, Fred Koenig, reminded me how important it is to concentrate in right. You might go four games without a tough chance, but then you might get one with a game on the line." Brewer rightfielder Charlie Moore, another former catcher, agrees. "I keep awake by either talking to myself or my centerfielder: 'I'll cheat toward the line, so come by me.' As a catcher I used to go crazy seeing balls drop in front of the outfielders. As a result, I play in close and work on balls hit over my head. I also have a pretty good idea how we'll pitch the hitters. I look where our catchers are setting up and guess what they're calling. As I guess, I cheat a little to my right or left."

What all rightfielders share is the dread awareness that theirs is an unforgiving position. After being tutored by Kaline to grip the ball by the seams and throw overhand, Kirk Gibson made an excellent throw to help Detroit win the first 1984 Series game. "A year ago I would have thrown a screwball," he said. A day later Gibson made two errors. Tony Gwynn spent the 1984 season building a reputation as a competent fielder. Then he contributed to allowing the go-ahead run of the last Series game when he lost a fly ball in the lights.

Waiting for plays—and he waits longer than anyone in the game—the rightfielder wonders what will go wrong. And something unfortunate, even ludicrous, happens all too often. In 1984 White Sox rightfielder Harold Baines was victimized by a blooper bouncing off the artificial turf in Minnesota's Humphreydome. When Baines charged the blooper too hard, the ball bounced over his head and carried to the fence for a three-run, game-winning homer. It could have happened anywhere in the outfield; it happened in right. In 1982 the Cubs' Moreland dived for a ball, got up, and couldn't find it. The ball was lying in his cap. It could have happened anywhere; it happened in right. And back in 1934, Hall of Fame centerfielder Hack Wilson was winding down his career as a rightfielder with Casey Stengel's Brooklyn Dodgers when a memorable afternoon in Philadelphia almost finished him. The hard-drinking Wilson, "hung over like a cornice," in the words of the late Red Smith, was running down line drives hit off Brooklyn's appropriately named Boom Boom Beck. Each time Stengel visited the mound to change pitchers, Beck talked him out of it. As they debated, the panting Wilson put his hands on his knees, lowered his head, and caught his breath. Finally, after one line drive too many, Stengel stormed to the mound and asked Beck for the ball. Furious beyond words, Beck wheeled and threw it to deep right. Wilson, who had been leaning against the fence and dozing, heard the familiar rattle of ball against wall. He wheeled, fielded the carom, and threw a strike to second. "That was the best throw Hack made all year," Stengel said later. Wilson could have been hung over anywhere; he was hung over in right.

By all odds, right has had the most colorful history of any position in the outfield. At first, admittedly, it was the weak spot on the diamond. There were few lefthanded batters, and pitchers threw so slowly that most balls were hit to center or left. The man placed in right was often the "change" pitcher, an early term for reliever, since teams were forbidden to substitute from the bench. Hall of Fame pitcher Old Hoss Radbourn spent an afternoon in right in which he won an 18-inning game with a homer.

Another oddity: right tended to be the "short" field, and shallow-situated rightfielders could always hope for 9-3 assists. On June 12, 1880, Worcester rightfielder Lon Knight threw to first baseman Chub Sullivan to retire Cleveland runner Bill Phillips and enable John Lee Richmond to throw the first perfect game in baseball history. The 9-3 play would continue sporadically through baseball history, featuring such luminaries as the Phillies' Chuck Klein, who in 1930 had 44 assists in tiny Baker Bowl (never were an outfielder and a stadium better suited for each other), and Brooklyn's Carl Furillo, who played Ebbets Field like his bedroom. The phenomenon didn't fade until the 1960s, when outfields became so large that even ven-

Two stars of the 1920s: Hack Wilson, above; and Sam Rice, right. *National Baseball Library*

turesome rightfielders had to station themselves prohibitively far from first. Nonetheless, Van Slyke worked the play on Atlanta pitcher Len Barker in a 1986 spring training game.

Whatever the shortcomings of the position, right field never lacked for characters. There was none wackier than Hall of Famer Michael Joseph (King) Kelly, who played for six teams in three leagues between 1878 and 1893. Kelly used to hide baseballs behind him in the long grass. If a hit arched over his head, he'd simply run back a few steps, take a ball from his personal collection, and throw it in. Once, when a tie game was concluding amid deepening shadows, Kelly heard the sound of a long

National Baseball Library

drive. He jumped, grabbed with both hands, and shouted joyously. Whereupon the game was called. They never did find the ball.

In 1891 free substitutions were permitted, and teams stopped using pitchers in right. One of the leading rightfielders of the time, the Phillies' Big Sam Thompson, changed outfield play forever by perfecting the one-bounce throw home; previously all outfielders threw only as far as the infield. Thompson played his last game in 1906, three seasons before Harry Hooper played his first for the Red Sox and six years before he made his famous World Series catch.

Thirteen years later came an almost identical play—and

the most controversial moment in World Series history. With Washington leading Pittsburgh 4-3 in the eighth inning of the 1925 Classic's third game, the Senators' Sam Rice vaulted into the temporary bleachers of old Griffith Stadium to take a homer away from Pirate catcher Earl Smith. Rice remained in the stands for some time before emerging with the ball. The Pirates and their owner Barney Dreyfuss charged onto the field, claiming that Rice had caught the ball, dropped it, and had it handed to him by a fan before emerging on the field. Some 1,600 fans provided affidavits, equally divided between Rice's supporters and detractors. Asked by the commissioner, Judge Kenesaw Mountain Landis, if he'd caught the ball, Rice said, "Judge, the umpire said I did." Landis judiciously replied, "Sam, let's leave it that way." And Rice did, at least until 1965, when he gave the Hall of Fame a sealed letter to be opened upon his death. In it Rice said he had a "death grip" on the ball but while falling into the stands "hit my Adam's apple or something, which sort of knocked me out for a few seconds." Eventually he was pulled back onto the field by centerfielder Earl McNeely. "At no time did I lose possession of the ball," Rice insisted.

Though Fenway Park's Green Monster was built in left, right was frequently the wall field in other parks. In the 1930s Mel Ott played the Polo Grounds wall with the same distinctive flair as he batted. Paul Waner and Clemente mastered both the fence and screen, which was in play at Forbes Field. Furillo played caroms off the Gem razor blade sign in Ebbets Field and threw to second so unerringly he was called The Reading Rifle. Later on, the selfless Al Kaline, who never took his hitting woes onto the field, made a game-saving catch while breaking his shoulder. Heartbreak? To many students of right field there's none greater than seeing the late Roger Maris left out of the Hall year after year. Forget about his seven World Series, two Most Valuable Player Awards, and one asterisk. He was a great defensive rightfielder as well. Just ask Willie Mays, robbed of a game-tying RBI when Maris held him to a double in the last game of the 1962 Series.

Even lesser rightfielders have had their days. The normally lead-footed Lou Piniella made two critical plays in the Yankees' 1978 playoff win over the Red Sox. In the sixth his running catch ("lucky grab" to diehard Red Sox fans) robbed Fred Lynn of a probable two-run double that would have given Boston a 4-0 lead. In the ninth, with the Yankees ahead 5-4 and Rick Burleson on first, Piniella alertly faked catching a Jerry Remy fly he

Pardon me, ladies! The Yankees' Roger Maris comes down on the wrong
side of the wall after his tremendous catch. Doubtless Maris is in violation
of the American League rule posted on the adjacent bullpen wall: "Players
in uniform must not talk with spectators before or during game."
National Baseball Library

had lost in the sun. Piniella caught the ball on a bounce, and
Burleson had to stop at second; if he'd advanced to third, he
would have scored on Jim Rice's subsequent fly to right-center.
Credit Piniella's "deke" ("blind stab" to Bosox boosters) with
the one-run margin of victory. Everyone concedes that Ron
Swoboda made the decisive diving catch of the 1969 World Series (even New York centerfielder Tommie Agee, who had two
great catches of his own).

It's somehow fitting, though, that the greatest play of the
greatest game in World Series history should have been made by
Boston's Evans, the nonpareil rightfielder of the post-Clemente
era and possibly the last of a noble breed. Like so much else in
our society, right field is becoming standardized, almost plastic. The old right fields had varying lengths of grass and dimensions, not to mention screens, fences, walls, funny angles, and
crazy corners. Whether the rightfielder stood close to the infield or far off, he was always better known for the quality of his
arm than his speed. Alas, the new parks usually have artificial

turf, walls eight to 12 feet high, and uniform dimensions (typically, 330 feet to the right- and left-field foul poles and 400 feet to dead center). Rightfielders no longer play tricky caroms or disappear into bullpens behind the stands. True, the fast turf requires the rightfielder to station himself deeper than he'd like to be and forces him to make longer throws. However, the carpet also speeds up base hits in the gaps and requires more speed than ever in right too. Forced to choose between fast legs and a strong arm—there are few Dave Winfields with both—most managers are tempted to opt for speed. As a result, the big guy with the catapult arm is in danger of being replaced by the little guy with roadrunner feet—frequently a displaced centerfielder.

Oh, there are still some rightfielders built along the classic lines, but they're often wasted on PhonyTurf: Minnesota's Tom Brunansky, Toronto's Jesse Barfield, and Cincinnati's Dave Parker spring to mind. For an old-fashioned rightfielder and an old-fashioned right field, we look to Evans.

Like his distinguished predecessors—among them Harry Hooper, Jimmy Piersall, and Jackie Jensen—Evans has grown to relish playing baseball's toughest right field. In Fenway, right is a difficult sun field because of the low grandstand. There are hockey-style caroms off a curved corner beginning 302 feet from home at the pole and extending to 380 feet in straightaway right. Balls are more likely to be hit over the low fence than off it, and there's virtually no foul ground. Evans learned to play right so well he would go 191 consecutive games without committing an error. Why shouldn't he have been the man of the moment in the 1975 Series' unforgettable sixth game?

In the eleventh inning Cincinnati's Ken Griffey was leading off first when Joe Morgan slammed a vicious shot to deepest right. It was a play every outfielder dreads—a liner directly over his head. If uncaught, Morgan's drive would have fallen for an extra-base hit or homer and almost certainly would have clinched the Series for the Reds. Many outfielders would have understandably dreaded the challenge that confronted Evans. Not he. "The worst thing an outfielder can do is fear a ball," he says. "I always hope they'll hit it to me."

Unlike the flashy players who misjudge balls, get late starts, and have to dive, Evans prides himself on making his best catches look easy. Sizing up Morgan's liner, he retreated quickly, eyes on the ball, leaped, and stabbed it as he crossed the warning track. "Given its significance," said shocked Cincinnati mana-

Boston's Dwight Evans, clockwise, fielding a base hit, getting set, preparing to throw, and firing to second base. *Matthew L. Kaplan*

ger Sparky Anderson, "it was one of the two greatest catches ever made." At the very least, it ranked on a par with other celebrated World Series catches by outfielders: those made by Ron Swoboda in 1969, Sandy Amoros in 1955, Willie Mays in 1954, Al Gionfriddo in 1947, Rice in 1925, and Hooper in 1912.

But there was more to Evans's play than the catch. Recovering quickly after fielding Morgan's blast, Evans threw toward a crowd of Red Sox uniforms. His quick release more than atoned for his imperfect aim. First baseman Carl Yastrzemski took the throw some 25 feet from the bag and relayed to shortstop Rick Burleson, who had crossed the diamond and reached first well ahead of Griffey. It was a 9-3-6 double play, if you're scoring, and a play that had fans, television viewers, and even sportswriters embracing and shouting, if you're remembering.

Remember this: Some of baseball's best moments come right out of right field.

"You wanta play?"
"More than anything in the world."
"Well, guys, it looks like we got ourselves a rightfielder."
　　　　—From the last scene of "Diamonds."

ROBERTO CLEMENTE

There was another landslide election in 1984. Responding to an informal poll, scouts, managers, coaches, former teammates, and opponents overwhelmingly selected the late Pirate Roberto Clemente as the greatest defensive rightfielder they'd seen.

They remember him in a series of surrealistic stills:

Clemente, spiderlike, back to the plate, climbing the Astrodome fence. His body is outlined against the yellow home run stripe eight feet off the ground. The date is June 15, 1971. Clemente has just made a game-saving, one-handed catch of Bob Watson's line drive. A moment later Clemente will crash into the fence and suffer a bruised left ankle, a swollen left elbow, and a bloodied left knee. And hang onto the ball. "Best catch I've ever seen," Astro manager Harry Walker said at the time. Bill Mazeroski, a Pirate second baseman from 1956 to 1972, wasn't so sure. "This was a lot like the one Roberto made off Willie Mays in 1961," he said.

Clemente, suspended horizontally three feet off the ground, his body at right angles to home plate. He has just made the kind of play he's best remembered for—fielding a hit at the line, spinning around, and leaving his feet while throwing to second or third. Clemente could also play caroms off the fence and hold runners to singles. He once caught a fly 420 feet from home and threw out a runner who had tagged at third. "I saw someone hit a fly to short right," says longtime Cincinnati first baseman Tony Perez. "Lee May was leaning on the third-base bag. Clemente got the ball on a *bounce* and threw out Lee by three or four feet at home."

Roberto Clemente leaps high—but this time not high enough to spear the Giants' Tito Fuentes's home run ball for the Pittsburgh Pirates in 1971. Note the outstretched right arm. *UPI/Bettmann Archives*

Clemente fielding a bunt! With runners on first and second and the Pirate shortstop covering third, Houston's Bob Lillis bunted through the shortstop hole. Clemente raced over from right, fielded the ball in short left-center, and threw out base-runner Walt Bond, who was attempting to go from first to third.

Clemente sitting up or lying face-down. He has just made one of his innumerable sliding catches.

Clemente, reeling, like a man who has just been shot. A ball he has lost in the lights has just hit him in the chest. He will recover to catch the ball before it hits the ground.

Clemente himself is not pictured in the final still. There's just a ball flying over the right-field stands in Forbes Field. "Orlando Cepeda of the Giants hit a line drive down the runway and past the bullpen, which was behind the stands and out of sight," recalls Phil Dorsey, a Clemente confidante. "Roberto picked up the ball and threw out the baserunner, Mays, at the plate. Damndest play I ever saw on a ball field." But not a unique one for Clemente. On other occasions he went into the bullpen to make blind throws and catch Cincinnati and Houston runners at third.

As a high school player Clemente switched from shortstop to the outfield. When he was 18, the Dodgers were conducting a tryout for 72 youngsters at Sixto Escobar Stadium in San Juan, Puerto Rico. "The first thing I did at the workout was ask kids to throw from the outfield," Dodger executive vice president Al Campanis recalled years later. "This kid Clemente throws a bullet from center, on the fly. I couldn't believe it. *'Uno mas!'* I shout, and he does it again. Then we have them run 60 yards. The first time I clock him he does it in 6.4 seconds—in full uniform. *'Uno mas!'* I shout, and he does it again."

The Dodgers eventually signed Clemente for a $10,000 bonus, left him unprotected on their Montreal farm club,[1] and lost him to the Pirates, who drafted him on November 22, 1954. As a big-league rightfielder in 1955–72, Clemente won 12 Gold Gloves and a league outfield mark of five assist titles. Players referred to his arm as El Bazooka. Its accuracy he attributed to throwing the javelin in high school, its strength to his mother. "She could throw a ball from second to home with something on it," he once said. "I got my arm from her."

"I remember Roberto coming out early to work on his throwing," says Phil Dorsey. "He'd set metal baskets on their sides at second and third. A coach, Ron Northey, would hit balls off the screen and Roberto would work for hours retrieving them and throwing them into the baskets."

"Clemente was to right field what Ozzie Smith is to shortstop," says Lillis. A fitting slogan for a landslide winner.

---

1. Because they had exhausted their unofficial "racial quota" of five minority players: Sandy Amoros, Jackie Robinson, Roy Campanella, Junior Gilliam, and Don Newcombe.

14

In Fairness to Fielding

The Braves were on the verge of breaking open the game on July 19, 1985. They were leading 1-0 in the seventh, with runners on first and second and one out, when Rick Cerone sent a hard grounder toward the left-field corner. One, maybe two runs would score, and a pitcher's duel would disintegrate.

Met third baseman Howard Johnson had other ideas. Dropping into a split position like some hockey goalie, he gloved the grounder for the save of the game. Ball in hand, Johnson rose and spun all the way round, first facing the outfield, then second base. I could swear he was laughing now. With plenty of time, Johnson threw easily to second baseman Kelvin Chapman to start an inning-ending double play.

The players ran off the field, and suddenly Shea Stadium was rocking. The PA system blared "Take Me Out to the Ball Game." The fans stood and sang, and when the music stopped they began a chant of their own. From everywhere it came: "Let's Go Mets! Let's Go Mets!"

Was I the only person in the park whose eyes were growing misty?

Defense will do that to me. The mere act of playing catch will move Kansas City reliever Dan Quisenberry. "Here's one of the primary attractions of baseball," he said one day, throwing a ball around with teammate John Wathan. "It soothes the mind and rewards the spirit. It's always fun. I guess it brings back what we were like when we were kids."

And what *were* we like as kids? Well, the first cherished possession we owned may have been a baseball glove. We opened a present and discovered the thing—a stiff strip of leather. We applied neat's-foot oil, caressing the glove, shaping it. And, lo, we created our first, primitive sculpture.

Gloves have evolved with the game, and their inventors and

experimenters should be honored among baseball's heroes. Most historians credit St. Louis first baseman Charles C. Waitt with wearing the first glove in 1875—actually, two flesh-colored gloves with the fingers cut off on his right hand to allow him to throw. Two years later Al Spalding, the founder of the famous sporting goods store, wore a black mitt to handle throws at first for the Chicago Cubs.

Soon everybody was using gloves, if those lifeless shards of horsehide could be so identified. Ah, but in 1919 Bill Doak, a righthanded spitballer for the Cardinals, brought gloves into the modern era. He approached executives of the Rawlings Company sporting goods plant in St. Louis with some revolutionary ideas—a preformed pocket in the glove, a webbing between the thumb and index finger. The next year baseball was transformed entirely. There was a new, lively ball, and a modern glove to catch it with.

The glove kept evolving. In 1922 a minor league player named Harry (Bud) Latina joined Rawlings as an assistant sales manager and began a family glove dynasty. Latina, who eventually became known as the "Glove Doctor," held more than 30 patents on sporting goods equipment, mainly gloves.[1] When he retired in 1960, his son, Rollie, stayed on. Under the Latinas the round catcher's mitt with the small pocket adopted a large crease and webbing. The first baseman's mitt developed from an oblong "trapper" model into today's rounder fly-catcher. Horsehide gave way to cowhide; today most mitts are made of leather, some vinyl. Infielders still wear relatively small gloves they can quickly dislodge balls from, while outfielders have gone to veritable man-eaters (Len Dykstra's glove looks bigger than he is!). And everywhere, gloves changed the style of play. Today's models are fielding machines. One can merely stick them in the face of a grounder or fly and legitimately hope to make the play. Hence, the greatest change in modern fielding: the one-handed catch.

Fielding was always something special. It's the most American subculture of our most American game. It's all wrapped up in our pastoral myth. What is fielding, after all, but play on fields—Elysian fields stretching forever to the frontier. It's territoriality—left field, right field, center field, infield, outfield.

---

1. When William Curran, the author of *MITTS*, asked him to name his favorite, Latina replied, interestingly, the Ed-U-Cated Heel. This little-noted patent replaced the open heel with the modern snug and contoured one that virtually prevents line drives from tearing gloves off fielders' hands.

It's the military necessity of defending bases (the most precious, of course, being home base). And above all, it's freedom and imagination. Anything can happen when a baseball is put into play, and what does happen sometimes defies credibility. Ozzie Smith strains every boundary of physiology at short. Those beeline throws from the right-field corner to third laugh in the face of gravity. Fielding is an infinity of possibilities, some of them seemingly impossible: the very promise of America.

More than anything, though, fielding is the glue that holds baseball together. My all-time favorite fielder, former Pirate second baseman Bill Mazeroski, knows this better than anyone. "Without defense, you aren't going to win," he says. "If you can't stop the other guy from scoring, you aren't ever going to score enough."

Ah, but preventing runs from scoring is the real joy of the game. "The term 'Classical Baseball' means simply, defense—all actions in the game of baseball except hitting and running are defensive," a Rochester English professor named Bernard Schilling wrote in the April 6, 1973, *Campus Times*. "What is a 'perfect game' in baseball? It is a defensive classic in which no one reaches first base—one in which not a single effort of the offense succeeds."

Just as the founder, old Alexander Cartwright, intended.